Yobbo Nowt

First published 1978 by Pluto Press Limited
Unit 10 Spencer Court, 7 Chalcot Road, London NW1 8LH

ISBN 0 904383 76 8

Designed by Tom Sullivan
Cover designed by David King
Cover photograph of Chrissie Cotterill by Beeban Kidron

Printed in Great Britain by Latimer Trend & Company Ltd, Plymouth

John McGrath

Yobbo Nowt

Pluto  Plays

Yobbo Nowt

Before writing *Yobbo Nowt* for the English 7:84 Theatre Company, I had just worked with them on a highly didactic entertainment about the multi-national corporations, called *Lay Off*. After discussion, we decided to attempt a more personal story in the form of a musical comedy, to tour with, and be a contrast to *Lay Off*.

Brecht's adaptation of Gorki's novel *The Mother* tells the story of a work-ing-class woman's growth to political consciousness and militancy in Russia at the beginning of this century. I had for some time been interested in telling a similar story set in England in the 1970s. We had all met on our travels many women who were going through a similar process. The story, of course, turned out to be almost completely different from Gorki's. But these were the sources, literary and real, from which came the story of Marie.

In form it is not exactly a musical comedy – though it is definitely musical, and a comedy. With Mark Brown, who composed the music, I set out to explore several ways of relating music to speech and story-telling: the sung narrative, straightforward character- and situation-songs, plus scenes in which the characters cut from speech to song, and scenes completely set to music. In this we were greatly aided by the presence in the company of some fine musicians and some excellent actors with good singing-voices, who had worked with us before on *Lay Off* and *Fish In The Sea*.

Yobbo Nowt toured with 7:84 for almost a year, and we all learned a great deal from the response of our audiences, in England, Wales, Scotland and Holland. It was then performed by the Liverpool Everyman Company under the title *Mum's The Word*.

On looking at the show again, one feature of comparison with both Gorki's novel and Brecht's play is striking. In telling this story today, we could not show Marie's learning experiences as including the vital strength of a coherent mass marxist movement. It would have been unrealistic to pretend that they would. We know from our own experience, and that of the many people like Marie whom we meet throughout Britain, that such a movement is our greatest need. It is to this movement of the future, and to all those in the company, and who have helped the company, that I dedicate this play.

J. McG.
March 1978

YOBBO NOWT by John McGrath
with music by Mark Brown
as presented by 7:84 Theatre Company (England)
on tour 1975–6

Marie	Chrissie Cotterill
Jack	Dennis Charles
Stephen	Colm Meaney
Val	Vari Sylvester
Narrator-singer	Hilton McRae
Narrator-singer	Harriet Walter
Tommy	Mike O'Neill
Alma	Harriet Walter
David	Hilton McRae
Mrs Harrison	Harriet Walter
Seymour	Hilton McRae
Mr Pugh	Dennis Charles
Josey	Harriet Walter
Frances	Vari Sylvester
Potshot	Mike Barton
Lady Spike	Harriet Walter
Cleghorn	Dennis Charles
Miss Williams	Vari Sylvester
Rev Chris Plum	Hilton McRae
George	Colm Meaney

Band:

Drums (plus piano and bass)	Chas Ambler
Keyboards	Mike O'Neill
Bass (and violin)	Mike Barton
Guitar (and banjo)	Tony Henderson

Directed by John McGrath
Musical Director, Mark Brown
Administration, Sandy Craig
Lights, John Tindale
Stage Management, Terry Dalzell

Act I

A kitchen. Early morning. As the song goes on, MARIE *comes on, then* JACK, *her husband,* VALERIE, *daughter, and* STEPHEN, *her son. They bolt breakfast and go.*

MARIE'S BALLAD

Singer   The time is pushing seven thirty –
The place a grotty town
Where folks are clean and weather's dirty
And life's all grey and brown
               – grey and brown

Our heroine's a normal mother
With Jack, her normal man,
For Val, her lass, and Steve her brother
She does the best she can –
Chorus   But she's a nobody
    A nobody
    Nothing to shout about
Now everybody's
    Somebody –
    But she's just yobbo nowt – yobbo nowt.
Singer   She lights the fire, she dumps the ashes,
    Puts breakfast on the plate,
She brews the tea, and clears the dishes,
    Makes sure they're not too late –

And as they go into the morning
    To work, to school, to life,
She sits there empty, lifeless, yawning –
    She's just a normal wife –

Yes she's a nobody –
    A nobody
Nothing to shout about
Now everybody's
    Somebody
But she's just yobbo nowt. Yobbo nowt. Yobbo nowt.

Kitchen. Remains of breakfast. MARIE *on her own, slumped at table. Desolation.*

Marie (*sings*)
>Blanketty – doo doo doo
>Blanketty – ah ah
>>My mind is a blanketty blank – oh oh

>Wednesday – doo doo doo
>Ten to eight – ah ah
>>My mind is congealed on a plate – oh oh

BAND *repeats above quietly as she speaks to audience.*

Marie Hell. I must get moving. (*Tries*) I can't I'm knackered. (*Tries teapot – it's cold, but she pours another cup, and doesn't drink it.*) Even the tea's got no warmth left in it. And the fire wouldn't light this morning. And the bacon's all froze together like stripey toothpaste.

STEPHEN *crosses on his way to school.*

Singer The kids have shot off to school
>Dribbling tin cans down the street,
>They're tactical, commanding and cool –
>Einsteins with brains in their feet . . .

VAL *and* ALMA, *her friend, on way to school.*

>The girls upstairs on the bus
>Craftily sneak drags on their fags –
>They're practical, commanding, no fuss –
>Queen's with their crowns in school bags –

Marie Blanketty – doo doo doo –
>Blanketty – ah ah
>>My mind is a blanketty blank – oh oh

>Wednesday – doo doo doo
>Every day – ah ah
>>The world is a light year away – oh oh

BAND REPEAT, *while:*

Marie I'm nobody. Yobbo nowt. All the rest of them seem to be up to something. Growing. Learning. Flirting. Mending fuses, making electricity hum. That's Jack – he started off as boilerman but he's doing night-classes and now he's going to be an electrical fitter in a plastics factory. He could get a job anywhere – as long as there's electrical juice shooting down the wires, they'll need Jack to see it on its way. Spurt. Spurt.

JACK *crosses on way to work, stops to wait for a mate.*

Singer Her man's off to work with bright eyes,
Whistling his tune as he goes
Brightening the grey morning skies –
Aglow with what only he knows.

His mate, TOMMY, *who looks grey and down, comes on yawning.*

Jack A'right Tommy? Grand mornin', man. Great to be alive . . .
Tommy Oh shut up can't you?

JACK *laughs secretly.*

What's puttin' a spring in your heel then?

JACK *laughs again, they go off together.*

Singer She turns and puts things away
Each packet in its proper place –
The dishes have nothing to say,
They stare back at her staring face . . .
Chorus Blanketty – doo doo doo –
Blanketty – ah ah
Her mind is a blanketty blank, oh oh
Marie Wednesday – doo doo doo
Ev'ry day – ah ah
I dream that I'm floating away – oh oh
Chorus She dreams that she's floating away . . .

NEVER BE THE SAME

Marie It wasn't always like this. Christ, no it wasn't. I just don't know what's
come over me – I think they must be right about the lead poisoning in the
water – makes you lethargic, and dull, and pathetic. But the others drink
the water. So it must be me. Perhaps I started life too young and I don't
mean at the early age of three weeks. I mean life. I was a woman when I
was twelve – them was the days –

She sings to audience, remembering.

SONG OF GETTING IT WHEN YOUNG

I was a woman when I was twelve
Goodbye the Beano and the Dandy

By thirteen years my head was full of men
Oh things will – never be the same.

For one long year I fought them off
Goodbye the Beano and the Dandy

But the men got bigger and the will was weak
Oh things will – never be the same.

Along came Tommy the electric man
Goodbye the Beano and the Dandy

With his port and lemon and his travelling van
Oh things will – never be the same.

So all you virgins hear my song
Goodbye the Beano and the Dandy

Love is lovely if you get it when you're young
And things will – never be the same.

Make your choice and take your pill
Goodbye the groping and the fumbling

And when you're ready for it, take your fill,
And nothing will ever be the same
No, nothing will ever be the same.

No. Nothing was ever the same. My ma found my diaphragm, chucked it away, and by the time I got another one, bingo – I was in the club. He had a sure touch, had Jack. Seventeen I was when I had our Valerie. And a married woman. I was lookin' at the wedding photos the other day – I look like a right gawky, lumpy kid.

We didn't get out together much, after that – well, there was the little girl, wasn't there? Jack had his night school, and sometimes a little bit more, I reckon. Where've you been till now? I'd ask him – Studyin' wirin'? But he only laughed, and he *could* have been out with the lads. You can't keep a man chained up in his kennel, can you? Not every night. But it was all right between us. It was lovely. Then along came our second, Stephen. That was when the trouble started. He was a right little sod, kept me up all night for months – and her round the house under my feet all day, and us trying to live in two rooms and a kitchen to get away from my mother's, and nappies and washin' and feedin'. No wonder it got on his nerves. I was like a wrung-out dishcloth when he came in at night, and he was still only a boilerman then, and he'd come in feelin' pretty flat. Aye, that was when the trouble started.

Singer A flashback to – 1961 – (*Flashback music*)

ARROWS OF DESIRE

Enter JACK, *a little bevvied. Hunts round for food, hacks himself a sandwich.* MARIE *watches him.*

Marie You bevvied?

Jack Ger off. Oops.

Marie Here. I'll cut that for you – what do you want?

Jack (*dirty laugh*) A slice.

Marie On your bread.

Jack Come here.

Marie Stop pullin' at me – I've had clammy little hands pulling at me all bloody day. (*Sniffs*) You smell like a whore's parlour – where've you bin?

Jack Leave off, will you?

Marie Well – who've you been with?

Jack No bloody body.

Marie See that. (*Fist*)

Jack I've been shovelling anthracite into a barrow, then out of a barrow into a boiler, then red-hot clinkers out of a boiler into a barrow, then off of a barrow on to a tip since eight o'clock this mornin'. I come in here for my tea and get blind hot pot and screamin' kids to set me up for an evenin' strugglin' through sums I don't understand, I get to the boozer and I can hardly lift the pot to my lips, and come home to – Where've you been? Who've you been with? (*Stands*) Get out my way.

Marie No, Jack, no, I'm sorry – don't go off like that.

Jack Well shut up then.

Marie Oh Jack – don't talk to me like that . . .

Jack Well what's the matter with you?

Marie Come on to bed.

Jack And what's going to bed with you going to do for me?

Marie I don't know what you want.

Jack Adventure.

Marie I'm tired.

Jack Excitement.

Marie You've been reading too many books.

Jack Fulfilment.

Marie All right – do what you like – but come on to bed before you wake the kids up with your shoutin' . . .

JACK *grapples greedily, brutally with* MARIE *on the table.*

BEDTIME

Singer   She goes to bed
           To look for sleep
           Unwind her mind
           From the day
           Her aching head
           Its secrets keep
           Her heart still starts
           Away

Her body craves
Some gentle touch
A kiss, a whis-
    per of care
A woman gives
A man so much
Then lies and cries
In fear

MARIE *gets up and goes to bed.* JACK, *disgruntled, watches her go.*

For all he gives is more demands
He's worked and worried too
A body tense he can't unwind
Some words he means but he can't find
The words he finds not true
The words he finds not true

JACK *goes off after her.*

With restless mind and restless hands
No tenderness no love
Too selfish scared to understand
He thinks she'll jump to his command
Not what she's dreaming of
Not what she's dreaming of

Chorus   Oh batter down the doors
Of the dungeon of desire

Girls   Fear is the padlock
We've thrown away the key

Chorus   Oh batter down the doors
Of the all-consuming fire

Boys   Passion is dying
And passion must be free

Girl Singer

Oh batter down the doors
Of the prison of true loving
Strong are the bars and
The bolt is thick and tight

All   Oh batter down the doors
Of the jail of true living
Shatter all the doors and
Escape into the light

Girl Singer

For night burns bright with flaming spears
When loving and passion and desire go free
But night clots black when lusts and fears
All stalk out hunting love and sympathy.

MARIE *comes back in, after unsatisfying sex, sits at table, eats a bit of bread, sad.*

Singer   The night winds weep
Outside the door
The room grows warm
As they lie
She longs for sleep
But sleeps no more
Once strong her longings die

Her body craves
Some gentle touch
A kiss, a whis-
   per of care
A woman gives
A man so much
Then lies and cries
In fear.

THANK YOU MA'AM

MARIE *shakes herself out of the past, lights change to now.* **To audience.**

Marie That's how it was for a bit. Then he stopped grabbin' at me – and I wished he would. Every now and again, we'd be in bed, and he'd just grunt, and wham bam thank you ma'am, all over. That's how it is now. Generally Tuesdays for some reason.

I want to get a job, but he won't have it. He says it wouldn't be a home, without a mother in it. But Stephen's at big school now, and Valerie's busting out all over her gymslip and they can look after theirselves a bit. Next autumn, I'll get a job. I'm only thirty-three; I must be able to do something. Right. I'm on my feet – must take advantage of that burst of energy. I'm going to do. Do you want to know what I'm going to do? It's really exciting. I'm going to make the beds, tidy the bathroom, hoover the landing, dust and hoover the stairs, hoover the hall, flick around the front room with a duster for five minutes, polish the door-knocker, sweep the doorstep, sweep the backyard. Some days I get really carried away and change the sheets. Then I can go shopping. That's all right. There's nice people in this part of town – they're friendly. Friendly in the butcher's, friendly in the grocer's, friendly in the bread-shop – not to forget the launderette. You'd think there was a friendliness competition. Chuck 'em in the river, they'd come up smilin' 'ee, love, you are a one – did you hear about Mrs Jenkins' daughter – glug glug glug – gasp – do you mi nd not throwin' them rocks at me, chuck, they're makin' a splash and I can't swim – glug glug glug – oh hello again – I think this is my last time, if I throw you my ticket, would you pick our Bill's shoes up from the cobblers? Thanks, love. Ta ta, nice seein' you – glug glug glug. Die.

Still it's better than misery. (*Goes*)

ALMA STRIKES

A street-light on a housing estate. Under it, a garden fence and hedge. ALMA, *waiting, a tall schoolgirl of seventeen. Awkward, but determined. Jaggy music.*

Alma It's mad. I bumped into him one night when he was coming back from night school and I was coming out of their house, and he walked me home. I could tell he was – on, you know – he asked me how old I was three times. The last time I said: I've told you. I'm seventeen. So it's all right. From then on it's been hedges and back-alleys three times a week. It's crazy. I'm going to school with his daughter – she's my best friend. At the moment.

Music in. She sings.

> I – can't – get that bastard out of my head –
> He's – just – fooling with me, wish he was dead –
>> I'm his screw
>> I'm his ride
>> I'm his bit on the side
>> But when he's
>> Right inside
>> Shit I nearly died
> He's a lover of a lifetime –
> And it's time-to-be-a-wife time
>> I want *his* kind of lovin' all of my days . . .
>> And I'm not going to lose him, no, no way . . .

I can't think about anythin' else. I'm supposed to be doin' A levels this summer, and going to university to do French. But I can't concentrate on Victor Hugo and Alphonse de Lamartine – they don't stay with you, that way. They don't thunder in your ears all night.

> I can't get that bastard out of my head
> I know it's all wrong, but – what's to be said
>> I'm his bird
>> I'm his lay
>> Something just to play (with) –
>> Every dog

Has his day – well
   I'm the bitch he's gonna stay (with) –
He's a lover of a lifetime
And it's time-to-be-a-wife time,
   I want *his* kind of lovin' all my days
   And I'm not going to lose him, no, no way.
   He's mine all mine and they can't take him away.

Enter JACK, *on his way home from work.*

Hello.
Jack Oh. (*Looks around*) Hello love.

ALMA *smiles.*

Jack What – er . . . What do you want?
Alma You.
Jack What – now?
Alma Later. My dad's gone to Stevenage to see about a job. My mam's gone with him to see about a house . . . I'm all on my own. I need protection.
Jack I'll give you that all right – here, but they'll be back won't they?
Alma Not before morning.
Jack Aye, well – look love . . .
Alma You be there. I'll be waiting.
Jack (*gleam*) Will you? Oho. But look, love . . .
Alma If you don't turn up, you can forget it. I mean that. But you will, won't you? I've been wearing lipstick on my nipples all day – just for you.
Jack Oh – I'll be there. If I can, Alma, if I can get away.

ALMA *smiles again.*

I'd best be off then. It's a bit – public here. I'll see you later. (*Pause, smile*) Hey – in a bed, eh? (*Down again*) I'll see you later then. If I can get away.

She watches him go.

Alma I don't think his wife appreciates him.

Enter VALERIE *on her way home from school.*

Hello Val – did you win?
Valerie It was only a practice – what you doin' walkin' the streets then?
Alma Been takin' pussy for a walk.
Valerie Dirty cow.
Alma Hey, your dad's just gone past.
Valerie Has he? I'll catch him up – Tara.
Alma Tara. (VALERIE *goes*) She's in for a shock, one of these days. (*Stops*) What am I doing? I'm frightened. (*Pause*) Never mind – moving to Stevenage soon.

Goes. MUSIC. *Back to kitchen.*

Music link to next scene.

BRAWN FOR TEA

MARIE *sits, still dreaming, nothing done.*

Marie I wish I had a cat. All over the world people are drowning kittens, and I haven't got one. Mother cats must go mad when people drown their kittens. All that work. And the milk – all pressing: must be really sore. The question is – should I have another kid? I'm not old, really – thirty-three. Nineteen seventy-five now – it would be twenty-four in the year two thousand. Valerie's sixteen now, so she'll be forty-one. Fancy her bein' forty-one. I wonder if she'll have learnt how to boil an egg?

In a certain light, our Valerie's eyes glint inside. No. I don't want a cat.

In burst JACK *and* VALERIE *together. They stand and look at her, and the empty table, with shock and horror.* MARIE *is flustered.*

Oh Christ, what time is it?

Valerie Where's the tea? I'm starving.

Marie I didn't know what time it was . . .

Jack We've got a telly, haven't we? Turn it on.

Marie They don't tell you the time on children's programmes.

Jack Look at this place. What have you been doing all day?

Marie Thinking.

Valerie There's nowt to eat.

Jack Thinking?

Valerie There's a tin of beans and some bread.

Jack What's that going to put in our bellies?

Marie Oh God, I just got moonin' –

Valerie (*scream*) There's no butter! We can't even have beans on toast.

Marie Where's Stephen? He normally tells me what time it is, he's got a watch.

Jack Excuses excuses. You haven't even done the shoppin'.

Marie I did, I did – it's in the basket – there's brawn, and pickles, and tomatoes, and a tin of rice pudding . . .

Jack A tin? Of rice pudding?

Marie And there's eggs – I could have them hard-boiled in a couple of minutes.

Valerie Eh?

Jack Thinkin'. Moonin'. How the hell d'you think it'd be if I let the boiler out, and the manager come round blowing his main valve and all I say is: I was thinkin'? How would that be, eh? How long do you think I'd last, eh.

Marie You get paid for your work – it's different.

Jack And you get kept. And clothed. And a roof over your head. And satisfaction – seein' your kids grow up.

Marie But I don't get satisfaction any more. I want to get out. I want to get a job.

Jack You've got a job. And you're not bloody doin' it.

Marie I don't like it, that's why.

Jack I'm none too keen on mine, love – as a matter of fact I fancy being an oil tycoon – (*Grunt*) You don't like it? That's unnatural.

Marie I'm going to get a job.

Valerie Will I serve this lot up then?

Jack Not for me, love, I've heard enough. I'll get a pie in the boozer . . .

Marie Going to the boozer? I'll come with you.

Jack Sod off.

Marie I will. I want to.

Jack You can't. You must feed the kids. That's your job.

Valerie Stephen's got football.

Marie If you go to the pub without me, you needn't bother to come back.

Jack EH? Right. I won't.

Valerie What's come over you two?

Jack You've made your bed – now you must lie in it.

Marie On me own. It'll be a pleasure.

Jack Don't kid on. You won't notice the difference.

Marie Oh yes I will.

Jack Val, go up and make the beds or something. I want to talk to your mother.

Valerie (*about to cry*) Stop it, can't you? Here, Ma – brawn, pickles, tomatoes, bread, butter.

Jack Go up them bloody stairs or I'll belt you.

Valerie (*to* MARIE) You cow. (*Goes, quickly*)

Jack Now. When I come back, I expect them kids fed, this place cleaned up, and you back to your senses. Or you'll get your cards.

Marie You've just had yours. Bugger off, and don't come whinin' back.

Jack Right. Then I won't come back. And don't think I've nowhere else to go.

Marie Oh aye.

Jack And a bloody sight more welcoming than you've ever been.

Marie Likely.

Jack And that. A good bit of that. Three times a night. (*Thinks*) Christ, I'm going to be free.

Marie Makes you feel a new man, does she?

Jack Don't you dare – don't you ever dare pour your sourness over her.

Marie Who is she, Princess Anne?

Jack Don't you care if I go off and leave you? Don't you care about the kids left without a father?

Marie No. I don't think I do. (*Sits*) I'm quite happy, sittin' here thinkin'.

Jack Oh. I think you've gone mad. Mental. Lost contact with reality. Marie – I am, I'm quite worried about you. Will I – get a doctor to you?

Marie (*quietly*, *seriously*) Piss off, Jack, before I slit you open with the bread knife.

Jack (*in awe*) You are – you're touched.

Marie (*quietly*) You heard me.

Jack I'm going. I'm not staying here with a ravin' nut-case.

Marie Go on then.

Jack I am. I am. (*Pause*)

Marie Who is she? Do I know her?

Jack She's very young. It's not going to be easy . . .

Marie Who is she?

Jack Alma.

> MARIE *checks, then roars with near hysterical laughter.* JACK *hits her, in anger, she screams. He goes.*

> VALERIE *immediately runs through shouting.*

Valerie Dad! Come back! Dad – she didn't mean it –

> *A pause.* MARIE *gets herself together, thinks, then giggles.* STEPHEN *comes in, his arm in a sling.*

Stephen What's goin' on?

Marie Your dad's gone away. For good.

Stephen Oh. (*Thinks*) I dislocated my shoulder. Sorry. (*Thinks*) Any tea, Ma, I'm starvin' – ?

> MUSIC *in.* SINGER *comes on in mock tragic pose.*

Girl singer
Calamity
Disaster
Chorus A woman without a man
Girl singer
Happily
Ever after –
Chorus That was nature's plan.
Singer Now if you're cool and sophisticated
With a mini and a bank account
Your life won't get too complicated
If your feller leaves the right amount
Chorus But she's a nobody
Nobody
Nothing to shout about
Now Everybody's
Somebody
But she's just yobbo nowt – yobbo nowt.

Singer   And if you're just a nobody
With cupboards clean but bare –
You learn the world's reality
As you fight to get your share

You learn the world's reality
As you fight to get your share.

ON HER FEET

Marie Amazing. He went. I didn't know I had it in me. If you just stop and think for a day, it's wonderful what you find you've got in you. What he did, he got himself bevvied and went round to Alma's. I don't know what joy he was copping from her, but it was rudely interrupted by her grandma who just dropped in to see if she was all right. Poor Jack – you haven't seen her grandma – she makes Mohammed Ali look like Twiggy. He got battered, Alma got battered, the neighbours were running for the bobby, Jack went scatterin' down the street in his underpants with his trousers round his neck, and some little lad swears there was bloodstains all the way to the bus-station. Word come back that Jack went off on the first bus, but where to I don't know, I've not seen hair nor hide of him since. And that was that. Except Alma's dad moved pretty sharpish to Stevenage, our Val had hysterics, and I'm left with two kids at school to feed, clothe, house and care for. And myself. Anyway, I've had my weep – well, it was only fair to him, to have a little weep – and now I'm on my feet, and I'm going to get a job. I'm looking forward to it. I'm going to do my bit for Britain.

Singer (*speaks*)
There was a man of double deed
Sowed his garden full of seed
When the seed began to grow
'Twas like a garden full of snow;
When the snow began to melt,
'Twas like a ship without a belt;
When the ship began to sail,
'Twas like a bird without a tail;
When the bird began to fly,
'Twas like an eagle in the sky;
When the sky began to roar,
'Twas like a lion at the door;
When the door began to crack,
'Twas like a stick across my back;
When my back began to smart,

> 'Twas like a penknife in my heart;
> When my heart began to bleed,
> 'Twas death and death and death indeed.

A GARDEN FULL OF SNOW

> MARIE *at the desk at the Labour Exchange.* DAVID *is getting impatient.*

David (*spoken*) Look, you've no stamps, you haven't even got a card, no experience, no training, you're a woman – and you want a job to support yourself and two kids.

Marie What's wrong with that?

David (*sings*)
> Mrs Arnold, you're having me on –
> The requests that you make are just crazy –

Marie (*sings back*)
> All I want is a job of my own – a job of my own – a job of my own
> I'm not dead –
> I'm not old –
> and I'm certainly not very lazy. I'm not lazy.

> I want to work somewhere where they make things – any sort of things –
> bars of soap, chewing-gum, warships, boots – something you can see. I
> don't mind what I do, as long as I know something's coming out the
> other end: then I can take my wages with a bit of pride.

David I see. Laundry work?

Marie Not if I can help it – I've been doin' washin' all my life.

David School meal service?

Marie Cooking or washing-up?

David Both.

Marie There again you see –

David Well we can't cater for whimsical requests, Mrs – er –

Marie Arnold. Yes, I can see that, and I'm in no position to mess about. Farewell fantasy number one. What pays best?

David (*sings*)
> Mrs Arnold, you don't understand –
> You just can't expect lots of money –

Marie (*sings*)
> All I want is some cash in my hand – (*He laughs*)
> It's not mad –
> It's not wrong –
> and it's certainly not very funny.
> It's not funny.

David
> How many times, oh how many times
> Have I heard the same demand,

But jobs today won't come your way
Just holding out your hand.

(*Brisker tempo, bolder*)

For boom-time is over,
Recession is here again –
Yes boom-time is over
For reasons –
I can't explain

The system's not working –
So you are not working too:
The system's not working –
There's noth-ing for you to do . . .

Marie Nothing? *Some* people get work – there's piles of people get work.

David I'm afraid, Mrs Arnold, when it comes to piles, you are at the bottom – of the pile.

Marie What about a shop? I know a woman got a job in a shop last week.

David A shop? I'll have a look . . . Well – there's one here looking for girls to train up – starting at eighteen pounds fifty a week – frankly, Mrs Arnold, though I shouldn't be saying this, a woman in your position would get more on the Social Security.

Marie No. I want to work. Even for that money.

David Very well – go to this address, and I'll make you out a card. Come back tomorrow please.

Marie (*looks at paper*) Marks and Spencers. Right.

MARIE *goes off.*

David   I send you out, to walk about
To trudge from door to door,
They pick and choose, you're bound to lose,
Not what they're looking for.

(*Spoken*) Next please.

Marie's Ballad tune in, on one instrument, quietly. MARIE *comes back on.*

Marie How is it, when they say they want us all to work harder for Britain, there's some of us desperate for work and can't get any?

When the man said the boom's over, he was right. I went to Marks and Spencers, this woman looked down her nose at me like I'd been dragged in by the cat. 'We want girls, smart young girls, to set off on the first rung of our ladder,' she said. 'I don't think you'd fit in to our scheme of things.' 'No,' I said, 'I'm not the climbing type' – and I give her a look. That was it – 'I'm awfully sorry, Mrs Arnold – I suggest you try the

agency from which we hire our cleaners.' That's one thing I'm *not* doing
– cleaning. Up at four in the mornin', knackered for the rest of the day,
and paid in washers.

I tried four mills – they laughed at me, they were laying off girls left right
and centre. I tried six more shops, the school dinners, Cadbury's, and
two chemical works. Nothing. You're a middle-aged, working-class
woman. Go away. After ten days, I'd run out of money, and I was fast
running out of patience. I went back to see the man.

Goes back into Labour Exchange. DAVID *again.*

David (*sings*)
>Mrs Arnold, you're breaking my heart,
>You just won't believe what I'm saying –

Marie (*sings*)
>All I want is to work for my keep,
>I'm not mad
>>I'm not dead
>>>and I'm certainly not simply playing . . .
>>>>I'm not playing.

David Mrs Arnold, I told you, I warned you. Just because you take it into
your head to do some work, you can't expect people to come rushing
forward with handfuls of fivers for your untrained, inexpert services.

Marie Well I don't – but there's so much needs doing, and I'm here to do it,
so why can't I?

David You people seem to think the capitalist system owes you a living – well
it doesn't.

Marie Is that what it's called?

David That's right.

Marie And it's the best we can think of?

David Yes – sometimes it needs people, sometimes it doesn't – and when it
doesn't – pht.

Marie But I thought it was good for everybody?

David Yes, but not all the time.

Marie Then it ought to be changed. I've got no money, and my kids won't
have anything to eat come tomorrow night, and the rent's not been paid
for a fortnight – it's not on, your capitalist system, how do you go about
changing it?

David (*shocked, then*) Well we've thought of something for people like you.
We take a lot of money from you when you *are* working, and give some
of it back to you when you're not. It stops you harbouring dangerous
thoughts.

Marie Well – do I get any?

David No. Unfortunately you don't qualify – no stamps.

Marie Oh for Christ's sake.

David Don't get extreme now, Mrs Arnold, be moderate in all things. We have another scheme for people like you.

Marie What's that?

David Social Security.

Marie Oh no.

David So take this form, and your blank new cards, and tell your whole story all over again to another man in another office, and he'll give you just enough money to stop you wanting to change the capitalist system.

Marie And if you hear of a job?

David Then you can *join* the capitalist system, and reap its benefits to the full – Bye bye.

Marie Have I upset you?

David You haven't upset anything, anything, Mrs Arnold. But keep trying –

Marie Bye then. (*Goes*)

Music in:

David (*sings*)

> How many times, Oh how many times,
> Have I heard the same demand –
> How many years, how many years,
> Before she'll understand – ?
> How many years, how many tears,
> Before she'll understand?

MARIE *comes on again, talks to audience.*

THE GREATEST OF THESE IS CHARITY

Marie Charity. What my family's fought tooth and nail to avoid. Charity's great for them that's giving it out – makes them feel good, a real Christian glow. But for them that's getting it – it can't do your pride much good. My dad said he'd rather beg than ask for charity. Still, Social Security isn't like going on the parish, and it is not quite the poorhouse. It's like all the people in the country saying: Ah, poor Marie Arnold, she's hit a spot of bother, we'll all club together to help her out till she's sorted. I think that's what it's like. Soon find out.

Singer

> In days gone by the charity
> Was crumbs dropped from their feast
> By those who caused the misery –
> The boss, the squire, the priest,
> But now, they say society
> Is equal just and fair –
> You learn the world's reality
> As you fight to get your share . . .

WHEN THE SNOW BEGINS TO MELT

Social Security Office. MRS HARRISON *looks up at* MARIE, *who sits opposite her.*

Mrs H. So your husband has run away and left you with no stamps on your card?

Marie Yes.

Mrs H. And two children at school.

Marie Yes.

Mrs H. And rent.

Marie Yes.

Mrs H. And several hire-purchase agreements.

Marie Yes.

Mrs H. And you can't find a job?

Marie No.

Mrs H. Hmm. Is there any reason he shouldn't pay you maintenance?

Marie Yes. We can't find him.

Mrs H. Have you informed the police?

Marie The police? God Almighty –

Mrs H. He should be paying you about twenty pounds every week he's away. In one year he will have deprived you of one thousand pounds.

Marie I don't want his money. I want to stand on my own two feet.

Mrs H. At the moment, Mrs Arnold, you are asking to stand on the taxpayer's two feet.

Marie Only till I can get a job. Let's leave Jack out of this.

Mrs H. He *is* your husband. In the eyes of the law he owes you a living.

Marie Oh.

Mrs H. Until such time as you take up with another man – then *he* owes you a living.

Marie Oh.

Mrs H. For all we know your husband is at home earning eighty pounds a week.

Marie You can come and have a look.

Mrs H. We will, Mrs Arnold. And we'll snoop around for signs of other men in your life. We'll go through your laundry for large woolly socks, we'll sniff the wind for potential co-habitors. And we'll track down your husband wherever he may be. To protect the taxpayer.

Marie Oh. In the meantime, do I get any money?

Mrs H. Come back tomorrow. And the day after. And the day after. And eventually, you might get a Giro. We won't tell you what you're entitled to. That's not policy. We'll work something out, and stuff it in your grasping hand. And you'll be grateful to the Welfare State, because otherwise you'd starve. And that we can't allow, not in a civilised country. Come back tomorrow, Mrs Arnold.

Marie Tell me something. Why am I your enemy?

Mrs H. The whole world is my enemy, because I deal in money and misery. For some, genuine need, genuine tragedy. For others, greed and cunning. Working out which is which – that makes everybody your enemy. But I am human. I have a husband, and a cat. I'm very fond of the cat. (*Smiles*) We won't let you starve, Mrs Arnold.

Marie No – you'll insult me, humiliate me, pry into my laundry basket and end up giving me just enough to keep me off the streets – how's that then?

Mrs H. (*sings*)

> In days gone by, Mrs Arnold,
> The weakest went to the wall,
> The pauper's grave, the poor house
> Disgrace to one and all –
>
> But poor men rise against their masters,
> Starvation leads to hate –
> If you've nothing to lose you'll risk it –
> So enter the Welfare State.

DAVID *comes on.*

David (*sings*)

> A state of almighty confusion
> A world of half true lies
> Where helping's a word for controlling
> And truth means compromise –

Both
> So don't be surprised if you're cheated
> By the hand that's supposed to feed –
> In the land where the rich speculator
> Is the judge of the poor man's need.
>   Fal-la-la – Fa-la-la-la.

THREE SLICES OF PIE

The kitchen. STEPHEN *eating toast.* VALERIE *doing homework.* STEPHEN *has black eye.*

Stephen I had three fights today . . . Two at dinner-time, one after school.

Valerie What for?

Stephen (*shrugs*) They're all taking the micky.

Valerie Let them.

Stephen Not out of me. Not even with one arm. (*Pause*) Do you know the difference between Kung Fu and Karate?

Valerie Oh shut up.

Stephen Karate is that. (*Business*) Kung Fu – is – that. (*Business*) I use a combination of both.

Valerie You'll get in trouble, you.

STEPHEN *laughs, eats.*

MARIE *comes in with a couple of paper bags.* STEPHEN *covers his black eye with hand.*

Marie I'm sorry I'm late, I had to walk to your grandma's and back.
Valerie What for? That's miles.
Marie It was her pension day today. I borrowed a couple of quid. Here, look, a feast: three slices of pie and a big tomato – what are you eating?
Stephen Dripping toast – great.
Marie Oh no – is that the end of the bread?
Stephen Er –
Valerie And the dripping . . .
Marie Stephen! Never mind. Slice that tomato up for us, Val will you?
Valerie Aw – I'm doing my homework.
Stephen Don't look at me, I've only got one hand. (*Reveals his black eye*)
Marie All right. What have you done to your eye?
Stephen Oh – er – walked into somethin'.

VALERIE *snorts.*

Marie What?
Stephen Just a goalpost . . . A goal mouth scrimmage. Here – do you want some bread? I forgot (*pulls a few tattered slices from his pocket*) I borrowed these from school dinners.
Marie (*upset*) You stole bread?
Valerie Christ. What have we come to?
Stephen I'm thinking of slipping some semolina in my pocket tomorrow, for you.
Valerie Shut up – stealing . . .
Marie It's not all that bad, Stephen – Here – dinner is served.
Stephen Could you cut it up for me, Ma?
Marie (*slicing his pie*) What's a Giro?
Valerie Something you take to the Post Office, for money.
Marie Is it? Oh – well I'll be getting one of those any day now from the Social Security. They'll be helping out till I get a job.
Valerie Oh no. That's charity. We're paupers.
Marie Of course it's not, love. You mustn't think like that.
Valerie And we're going to be thrown out on to the street –
Marie How do you mean?
Valerie The rent man came round, wanting twenty pounds. Said something about a court order. We're finished. Bankrupt. Begging for charity.
Marie No, we're not.
Stephen Stop making it worse. It's bad enough as it is, without making it worse.

Valerie She should never have sent him away.

Marie Shouldn't I?

Valerie She drove him out. She drove him out. Now we're all helpless – all because of you.

Marie No we are not. You don't seem to realise: it might be a bit hard, but it's very exciting: we're all three of us starting out on life, together. For the first time, we've all got to make our own way, and think for ourselves. If your dad come back through the door right now – I wouldn't want him. I wouldn't want to go back to four walls and a dishcloth. There's a big world out there, love, I want to be part of it. I want to see what's wrong with it, and what's right with it, and I'm finding out already. Listen: the dole-money and Social Security you think is charity. Well it's not. They've got a system going in this country that works great for some, and doesn't work so great for others; and they're frightened in case anybody notices. So if the system's mucking you about, they give you just enough to shut your mouth about it. And *then*, they pretend it's charity. That much I've found out. And I want to find out a whole lot more.

Valerie I want my dad back.

Marie Do you? Well, I'm sorry love, but he won't be coming – not for a long while.

Stephen What?

Marie I got a letter from him this morning. Four lines, no address. He's signing on a merchant navy ship – cargo run around the Pacific. Two years minimum. That's all he said.

Valerie That's *all*?

Marie Yes, love.

Valerie No love to nobody? No sorry?

Marie Nothing. Just that.

Valerie Right, well, I'm leaving school and getting a job. Bugger him.

Marie You don't have to do that.

Valerie I'm going to.

Marie You must sit your exams in June – you must.

Valerie All right. *Then* I'm going to get a job.

Marie Why?

Valerie He wanted me to go to university, didn't he? Well if that's all he cares about us – I won't. Now I'm going out. I've got someone I want to see.

Marie But –

VALERIE *goes.*

Marie Right, Stephen, it's you and me for the washing-up then.

Stephen Can *I* leave school, Ma?

Marie No you can't – you can wash and I'll dry.

They go off.

THE OLD DOCK WALL

Enter JACK, *with suitcase. Country and Western music. He puts down his suitcase, takes off his jacket, picks up microphone, strikes a pose, and sings:*

Jack	Now my heart is fit to break
	And my hand's begun to shake –
	For too long, I know, I've played the fool –
	Yes my tears begin to flow
	And my pain begins to grow
	For I'm lonely
	And I'm blue
	In Liverpool . . .
Chorus	Maggie May
	Has gone away
	And the streets
	Are cold and grey –
	Yes I'm lonely
	And I'm blue
	In Liverpool . . .
Jack	For my wife and kids I call
	As I walk that old dock wall:
	You were right, I've broke-en every rule,
	And as on that boat I sign
	For my home I start to pine,
	For I'm lonely
	And I'm blue
	In Liverpool . . .
Chorus	Maggie May, etc.
Jack	Oh who will be waiting in Honolulu,
	And what do I care, if that someone isn't you,
	And when I steam homewards to that berth up in the skies,
	I will pray to my maker you'll be there – in Paradise.

(*speaks*) Now I'm bound to travel this whole world over, but no matter where I roam, I'll never find anywhere as sweet as twenty-three A Clem Attlee Close.

(*sings*)

Now my boat is under way
And I curse that fateful day
And my heart is kick-ing like a mule –
For those tugs tug at my heart
And I know we shouldn't part
But I'm sailing
Far from you

And Liverpool
Maggie May
Has gone away
And the streets
Are cold and grey
As I'm sailing
Far from you
And Liverpool.

Thank you, country and western fans – thank you. A man's got to do what a man's got to do.

He goes off.

A SHY YOUNG MAIDEN

On one side of the stage a coin-box. VALERIE *goes into it, dials.*

On the other side, enter SEYMOUR, *a cool young man, spoilt, affected, self-confident, in very casual elegance; he carries a telephone on a long lead.* VALERIE *pushes coin into box.*

Seymour Hello?
Valerie Is that Seymour?
Seymour Hello Carol – fancy you ringing up –
Valerie It's not Carol, it's Valerie – Val Arnold . . .
Seymour Valerie – Val Arnold – fancy you ringing up.
Valerie Yeh, fancy.
Seymour Going to come round and see me?
Valerie Well – I might. One of these days.
Seymour Do you like horse-riding? We could try a canter together on the common . . .
Valerie I've never done horse-riding. (*Pause*)
Seymour Val?
Valerie Yeh?
Seymour What did you ring me about?

MUSIC *in.* VALERIE *takes a deep breath and explains.*

Valerie (*sings*)
My dad's gone off and left us
So we're short of ready cash
And when I met you at the Christmas Dance
You told me I was just the girl
Your firm was looking for –
And now I need the job – is there a chance?

Seymour Now listen little Valerie,
    You've a lovely speaking voice
      But I must confess I can't recall your face –
    I must refresh my mem'ry
    Of the freshness of your smile –
      So what about refreshments round my place?

Valerie But can I trust you Seymour,
    You're an awful flirt
    You've mixed me up already with
      Some other piece of skirt –
      You seemed a nice young chappy
      But if *you'd* be just as happy
    Could I meet you in the office
      Where there's none of us can get hurt?

Seymour (*aside*) Oh-oho-oho-oh-oh-OHO!
    Oh what a shy young maiden,
    I begin to feel intrigued –
      As I recall she'd lovely you know whats –
  (*To her*) How old are you now Valerie?

Valerie Seventeen come next July –

Seymour (*aside*) That voice is going to tie me up in knots . . .

Valerie So can I come and see you,
    I'd love to work for you –
      You told me that the prospects were quite good –

Seymour The prospect's very thrilling –
    Say tomorrow, half-past five,
    And I'll behave just like you think I should . . .

Valerie (*spoken*) Right. Half-past five. Brittania House.

Seymour Just ask for Mr Bell, Mr *Seymour* Bell – you don't want to end up talking to my dad, now do you?

Valerie Don't I?

Seymour I wouldn't. Bye now – (*Hangs up delighted with himself. Goes*)

Valerie Oh God – what have I done? (*Hangs up*)
  (*sings*)
    I'll be a business lady
    With a motor-car –
    I'm going to chat up clients
    In the cock-tail bar
    If Seymour treats me gently
    He can drive me in his Bentley
    I'll soon be rich and famous
      Yes I think I'll go quite far –

Chorus Yes she'll soon be rich and famous
      And she thinks she'll go quite far –
  She goes.

ONE THURSDAY IN JULY

MARIE *comes on and talks to audience.*

Marie Our Val's up to something. I don't know what – but I intend to find out. Suddenly she's best mates with half the girls in her class and *has* to go round to their houses for the evening – or the week-end. I hope she knows what she's doing.

Stephen's shoulder got better. And his black eye –

STEPHEN *enters, arm in a sling. Sees her, exits.*

Stephen!

Stephen (*comes back*) Hello, Ma – broke my arm. Sorry.
Marie How?
Stephen Pole-vault – missed the pit – great jump though . . .
Marie When I get you home, I'll break the other one.

STEPHEN *goes.*

He was a real comfort to me, all the same, was Stephen. The months slid by like sludge from a dredger. I got my Giro, every week. They wouldn't give it me in my hand. I had to go and prove I needed it desperately, then they'd prepare it, then when it was all ready, they'd show it me, then they'd post it. People began to pity me. You know what friendly people are like. Pity you in the butcher's, pity you in the grocer's, pity you in the bread-shop, not to forget the launderette. Oh, Mrs Arnold, I was that sorry to hear about Jack going off and leaving you – you need a man in your life, don't you? I imagine you'll all be very sad – but don't worry, at times of trouble, folks rally round – we'll see you all right. Thanks, missis, you're so kind, so friendly, don't step in that dog muck now. Oh dear, what a pity. Here, wipe it on my old coat, why don't you?

Then, one Thursday in July – it all began to happen . . .

DAVID *comes on.*

David (*sings*)
        Mrs Arnold, I've found you a job
        In a way, I'm quite sad, I shall miss you.
Marie (*sings*)
        At last you've found me a job of my own
           A job of my own.
           A job of my own.
           Don't be sad,
           I'm so glad
           I'm so happy I think I could kiss you.
                      I could kiss you.

She kisses him on the cheek.

David Don't do that, Mrs Arnold, it's against regulations. Anyway, you've got to satisfy the Personnel Manager first – but I'm pretty sure you'll manage that –

Marie What is it?

David Electronics. Mrs Arnold – you're to be burned up in the white heat of Technology. Two months training on half pay, then you're off into the cybernetic future – on piece-work. I've got a strong feeling your dreams are all going to come true – next Monday, you'll be joining the capitalist system. Good luck, Mrs Arnold, good luck.

Marie (*going*) Thank you.

David How many times, how many times,
    Have I seen their eyes a-glow –
    How many days, how many weeks
    Before her smiles all go?

Enter ASSISTANT PERSONNEL MANAGER, MR PUGH. *Meets* MARIE.

Mr Pugh Mrs Arnold?

Marie That's right.

Mr Pugh Any experience of electronics?

Marie No but I'm keen to learn – and to work.

Mr Pugh In a union?

Marie No.

Mr Pugh Political?

Marie No.

Mr Pugh Afraid of hard work?

Marie No.

Mr Pugh Right. Two months' training, twenty-one pounds a week – start Monday, seven-thirty sharp – bring your cards and your P forty-five to the office.

Marie Oh right – have I got the job then?

Mr Pugh I'm a shrewd judge of people, Mrs Arnold, and a man of decision. You'll work till you're dropping and cause no trouble – am I right?

Marie Oh – yes – you're right.

Mr Pugh I knew I was. Monday morning then. Hours – seven-thirty to four-forty-five, one hour lunch, ten minutes break in the morning, five in the afternoon, no smoking on the job. You're on.

David (*sings*)
    You're on, Mrs Arnold,
    The wheels are all turning now –
    You're on Mrs Arnold,
    Your keep you'll be earning now –

Producing, creating
And not just consuming now
Producing, creating
Your life's started blooming now

She goes over to MRS HARRISON.

Marie Well hello it's good-bye, Mrs Harrassment – you can stuff your Giro up your letter-box, I've got a job.

Mrs H. Oh, I *am* pleased to hear that, I really am – so is the taxpayer.

Marie I can have as many men as I like now, can't I? I can have the whole house seething with randy navvies – and you won't even look in my dirty washing.

Mrs H. No – you can cohabit with the whole fire brigade now if you don't mind the sudden emergencies – wonderful.

Marie Why are you in mourning?

Mrs H. Oh – it was the cat. Not gone from us but asleep.

Marie Oh dear.

Mrs H. Never mind – so long as somebody's happy – here – take this lot with you – au revoir, Mrs Arnold.

Marie Tara. (*Goes*)

David and Mrs H. (*together*)
Mrs Arnold, we hope that you win
Mrs Arnold, don't ever give in –
Mrs Arnold . . .

PORT AND LEMON

MARIE *comes into kitchen with carrier bag, all chirpy, puts bottle of port and some bitter lemon on the table – as she does,* VALERIE *comes in with identical bag, looks, laughs, produces the same.*

Marie What's that for?

Valerie What's that for?

Marie I've got a job.

Valerie So've I –

Marie Have you?

Valerie What's yours?

Marie Electronics – making colour telly and that –

Valerie Bloody hell – sounds complicated.

Marie I can't even mend a fuse, but they took me on. Twenty-one quid a week – for a bit – then the sky's the limit. What's yours?

Valerie Promotion.

Marie Already? You haven't even started yet.

Valerie No. I'm part of a team – three girls. We all get dressed up as rabbits, and knock on people's doors. When they open it, they're supposed to say: I recognise you as one of the bunnies from The Warren, then sing, Run Rabbit, Run Rabbit, to the Warren Club – and I reply Come and Grab It, Come and Grab It, Here's a year's free sub.

Marie Oh.

Valerie Well, they've supposed to have heard about it on Radio Valium – it's for this new Social Club, getting members.

Marie Oh.

Valerie If they don't recognise it, I try to sell them a year's membership, only four pounds fifty – I've got to learn three whole pages of what to say.

Marie How much do you get for that?

Valerie Fifty quid a week.

Marie And is that going to be your life's work?

Valerie It's for an agency – they get lots of jobs like that, all the time: I know the bloke who runs it – well, his son.

Marie Very nice, I suppose, very nice.

Enter STEPHEN *on crutches, with his leg in a plaster.*

Stephen I broke my leg, sorry.

Marie Wh – ?

Stephen Playing billiards. I fell out of the window. What's for tea?

Marie It's port and lemon tonight, love, with chips. We're celebrating.

Stephen Celebrating?

Valerie Me and your ma's got jobs.

Stephen What about me? Why can't I get a job?

Marie All in good time, lad. Sit down, and you can have some of this. Get the glasses, Val.

Stephen I'm the man of the house. I should be supporting you.

Marie Well, you can forget that idea, just for a start, we've had a man of the house. And there's a few more ideas going to change round here before we're through, eh Val?

Valerie Are there?

Marie There are. Come Monday, I'm joining the capitalist system, so look out, you managing directors – I'm on my way.

Valerie So am I.

Marie Here's to our future.

Valerie Right.

Stephen And the National Health Service – from its chief customer.

All The future.

As they drink, MARIE *produces fish and chips – and* STEPHEN *explains, to general merriment, how he fell out of the window – then pretends to be drunk.*

Singer   The future's looking pretty rosy
              In that old grotty town
          But nothing's ever quite so cosy
              Just take a look aroun'

For life's not long, to make it better
   She's got to shake that town
To make it better if the world will let her
   She must turn it upside down.

All   And she's a nobody,
Nobody,
Nothing to shout about –
Now everybody's
Somebody,
But she's just yobbo nowt, yobbo nowt – yobbo nowt.

END OF ACT I

Act II

Factory – women working on machines. JOSEY *and* FRANCES *sing-talk.*

Josey   Do you fancy Bruce
                For
                   Syth?

Frances Who?
Josey   Do you fancy Bruce
                For
                   Syth?

Frances Well I think he's got a lovely pair of legs
Not a hair upon his head is out of place –
He's got some clever patter
But it really doesn't matter
Cos I'd love to smash that grin right off his face –

Chorus Men, men –
They're ever so boring men –
  I don't know what we talk about them for –
Men men
Don't mention men again
  We won't discuss the bastards any more . . . No more.

Frances Do you fancy Park
                In
                   Son?

Josey   – Who?
Frances Do you fancy Park
                In
                   Son?

Josey   Well I think he's got a lovely speaking voice
And he makes you think he's ever such a chum –
  But he'd better take a rest
  Cos if I was his guest
I would stick his dirty snigger up his bum –

Chorus Men, men, etc.

NATURAL GAS

MARIE *comes in with* MR PUGH – JOSEY *and* FRANCES *speed up their work rhythm – backing beat speeds up with them.*

Mr Pugh Very good, girls, very good. If I didn't know you, I'd be impressed. All right – you can calm down. (*They stop*)

Frances Hello Mr Pugh.

Josey You're early Mr Pugh.

Mr Pugh Where's Alec?

Josey Gone to the store, Mr Pugh.

Mr Pugh Oh aye – well this is Mrs Arnold. (*To* MARIE) The chargehand's away, so these two'll get you started – show her the ropes, girls – and not the ones you swing the lead from. (*To* MARIE) Right, Mrs Arnold – I believe the average on these machines is thirty operations per minute – this lot manage about twenty, I expect you to be hitting forty by this afternoon – any problems, ask Alec.

MR PUGH *goes.*

Marie Hello. (*They nod*) What – what must I do?

Frances You get hold of that, squeeze it, and out shoots the stuff.

FRANCES *and* JOSEY *laugh.*

Marie Sounds familiar. Then what?

Josey Then you're in business. All you've got to do then is stamp your foot and do it again.

Marie Oh. All right – I'll try it.

Does.

Is that all right?

Frances Looks all right to me.

Marie What now?

Josey Just keep doin' it.

MARIE *carries on, the others watch. She gets carried away, faster and faster. She stops, pleased with herself.*

Frances You on piece-work?

Marie No – I'm on two months' – er – training . . .

The other two swing back to their machines, without comment.

Have I done anything wrong? (*No answer*) It's only two months anyway – *then* I go on piece-work.

The other two stop, look at each other.

Marie Oh God – now I've said something else. Look, will you two stop lookin' at each other and tell me straight – what have I done wrong?

Frances Well, to start with, you're already trained.

Marie There must be more to the job than *that* . . . ?

Josey Yes – you have to learn how to switch the switch on and off – that'll take all of ten seconds.

Marie Then why do they say two months training . . .?

Frances How much they paying you?

Marie Twenty-one pounds – only for two months.

Josey The last girl who worked that machine got twenty-one pounds for the two months – then they sacked her. And the one before.

Marie Oh.

Frances They're not stupid you know.

Marie They won't do that to me – that's daylight robbery.

Josey Won't they?

Marie *No.*

Frances So what if they don't? Then you go on piece-work – you've agreed that, have you?

Marie Well – yes. Well – he said I'd get paid according to how many I did.

Josey You see, we've been having a campaign for the last two years to put a stop to piece-work – we want a guaranteed wage and bonus system.

Marie Oh – I see. Surely, on piece-work, the harder you work, the more you earn – that sounds fair to me . . .

Frances And who suffers if there's a shortage of rods, or a delay in deliveries, or if you get a load that crack, or if your machine break down? Who's the first to suffer when the demand for these things drops? Not them love – us.

Marie Oh. Then they're not on. I'll go and tell Mr Pugh, he's not on.

Josey All right. If you want your cards before you've even started.

Marie My cards? Of course not – I'll just explain to him how unfair it is, that's all.

Frances Then what?

Marie Then he'll see reason . . . no, I suppose he wouldn't. Then what can you do?

Enter MR PUGH.

Mr Pugh What's this, what's this? Would you ladies kindly have your mother's meetings in your own time – no wonder British industry can't attract investment – there's more natural gas here than under the North Sea. Mrs Arnold – you're letting me down. I took you on because my instinct told me you were a good loyal worker. Don't disappoint me – will you?

Marie Mr Pugh – how come I get training money for two months, when it only takes ten minutes?

Mr Pugh Are you telling me how to do my job already?

Marie No, I'm asking –

Mr Pugh Well don't – you agreed to it, that's why.

Marie And did I agree to piece-work after?

Mr Pugh If you last that long – yes.

Marie I want to change my agreement.

Mr Pugh But there's nothing to change it to, Madame Arnold – that's our custom and practice, that's the way we do things. (*To* FRANCES *and* JOSEY) Where's Alec? Still in the store-room?

Frances Something like that.

Mr Pugh Right – I'll sniff him out. Watch your step, Mrs Arnold. We in Marriners Electronics, don't like trouble makers. (*Goes*)

Marie Christ Almighty – what a set-up.

Frances It's pretty normal.

Marie What can you do about it?

Josey Get on with it. Not too fast.

MUSIC *of 'MEN MEN' comes in. They all start work.*

Marie (*to audience*) Is this what I'm supposed to do for the rest of my life? I know, I know – I spent months hunting for a job, I was overjoyed when I got one, now I'm complaining after ten minutes. Well I *am* grateful for the money – such as it is. Well at least I'm producing things – though God knows what they are – (*To* FRANCES) Eh, what are these things for?

Frances They go into transformers.

Marie Oh. (*To audience*) They go into transformers, right? I'm glad to be helping transform things. But I've got a feeling I'm being conned – taken advantage of, just because I need the work. Perhaps we're all being taken advantage of, 'cos we need the work. I'll have to look into this capitalist system – I'm not at all convinced it doesn't need scrapping.

Goes back to work.

Josey Do you fancy – anybody at all –

Frances – Who?

Josey Do you fancy – anybody at all?

Frances Well I fancy havin' fellers that are big and strong
But most of them is vain and pretty thick –
   I fancy one that's gentle
   But most of them is mental
In fact I think they mostly make me sick.

Chorus Men, men, etc.

POTSHOT

At the end of the chorus, hooter blows, machines stop, and the three women go off and sit on the front of the stage, get out flasks of tea, etc.

Marie Are they trying to rob everybody?

Josey Just about – depends how you look at it.

Marie How many work here then?

Josey Four hundred odd.

Marie Then why don't we all get together and go and tell them we're not standing for it?

Frances We thought of that a hundred and fifty year ago. It's called a union.

Marie I suppose it is. Are you in a union?

Josey Yes. She's our shop-steward, her –

Marie Are you?

Frances Can't you see my horns and my spiky tail?

Marie Am I obliged to join the union?

Frances No, you're not. That's half the bloody trouble. If we could get a union shop in here, we'd stop them bastards conning people like you on this training racket, and we'd put a stop to the piece-work swindle, too – but half the girls won't join – just not interested.

Marie Oh.

Josey You going to take out a card then?

Marie Well I don't know . . .

Josey You was the one said we should all get together and go and sort them out, wasn't you?

Marie I was. But – don't you think the unions are the cause of all the trouble in this country? Inflation, strikes, all that?

Frances Suit yourself, love.

Marie I mean, aren't they all under the control of extremists out to destroy the country?

Frances Do you mean like Len Murray?

Marie You see – I don't know who he is, I'm ignorant.

Josey Don't worry, love, you'll find out.

Marie I'll think about it.

POTSHOT *crosses, pushing hand-trolley,* JOSEY *whistles. He stops. Goes on He is a young, enigmatic student.*

Josey Eh, Potshot – come here.

Potshot Begone. I am about my employer's business.

Josey Come here when you're told.

Potshot Do you promise not to say anything indelicate? My mother always warned me against ladies like you.

Josey This is our new girl, Marie.

Potshot Hello. Take no notice of me I'm a student.

Marie Oh. Hello. What are you a student of?

Potshot At the moment, stacking boxes. Very shortly, de-stacking boxes. Eventually, structuralist semantics.

Josey Isn't he sweet?

They giggle at him.

Marie's thinking about joining the union.

Potshot Ah.

Marie Do you think I should?

Potshot (*deep breath*) Marriners Electronics Ltd, as you no doubt know, is a wholly-owned subsidiary of Spike Electric, chairman and managing director, Sir Jules Spike.

Marie Spike?

Potshot Well, something sharp – a gentleman who lives in a large house in Guildford, Surrey. Turnover in nineteen seventy-three, five hundred million pounds; profit, seventy-four million pounds, number of employees, eighty-five thousand. Average profit per employee, nearly one thousand per year – that means they're making twenty pounds a week out of you, and you, and you. And me. Next year they intend to make more. How will they do this? I hear you ask me. They will attempt to produce and sell more goods, and pay the same wages. They will employ every trick in the bosses' book to cheat you of your share of the increase in the firm's prosperity, and yet make you work harder; they will try to achieve this by uniting with the other employers of this country, to attack the trade unions – which are the only organisations to defend the interests of you, the workers. And their main weapons in this attack are confusion and apathy. If you, Marie, are confused and apathetic, you have already given in to Sir Jules Spike, and he is laughing.

Josey Show us your legs, Potshot.

Potshot I shall disregard that. Now, this conspiracy of profiteers, usurers and parasites, i.e. industrialists, financiers and shareholders, form the backbone of the ruling class, and of the British State – which is more permanent and more powerful than any elected government, which, in fact uses governments, of whatever shade, as its servants. And this ruling class is quite clever. It may, in fact, concede some of the unions' demands, in the way of wage rises; and use them to justify price increases, which will further increase the profit, and make the higher wages actually worth less. In this way the capitalist system actually uses the unions to defeat the workers. Why then, join the union? Answer: to turn it into what it should be – a weapon to overthrow the entire capitalist system. Do you wish to do that?

Marie As a matter of fact, I do, yes.

Potshot Do you?

Marie Of course I do, it's a terrible system.

Potshot Then, comrade, you should join the union. Ladies – beware – you have a revolutionary in your midst. Mind your language.

POTSHOT *goes.*

Josey Here – are you a communist?

Marie Of course I'm not. I don't think so. I don't know what I am – I'm beginning to wonder . . .

Hooter, they go off, leaving MARIE, *who talks to the audience again.*

I got quite taken aback by the things I kept coming out with: they took me completely by surprise: not that I didn't mean them – I just didn't expect them. And they got me into awful trouble. Poor Mr Pugh, I just got it into my head one day to tell him that his job that he was paid for – was to rob and cheat people on behalf of the capitalist system, and as such was unworthy of a good Methodist Christian. He said I could have my cards, but I told him I was in the union, and he'd have to have a better reason for sacking me than a bit of friendly advice or they'd all be out. He swore – in Welsh. Now I've got to watch my step – one slip-up on the job and he'll have me out the door. But I'm on full rate now, getting about thirty-three a week, less this and that. So I intend to stay for a bit.

Our Val's working two weeks out of three as well, for this agency – she got eighty quid the other week – and she's started staying out till two in the morning – with Seymour, whoever he is. Sounds a right mardy clown, if you ask me.

As for Stephen – he thinks I've deserted him, poor lad. But he keeps himself amused . . .

PEACE BROTHER

The kitchen. STEPHEN *doing weight-lifting routine: powder on hands, etc.*

Stephen The greatest weight-lifter the world has ever seen is Vasili Alexeev of the USSR – holder of every super-heavyweight record. He lifted five hundred and eighteen pounds with one jerk. BUT Mrs Maxwell Rodgers lifted one end of a station wagon that had slipped off a jack and on to her son. It weighed three thousand six hundred pounds. She weighed eight stone eleven pounds. (*Lifts again*) Bloody hell. Paul Anderson of the USA raised two tons sixteen hundredweight off of trestles on June twelfth nineteen fifty-seven. Six thousand two hundred and seventy pounds. BUT the only man ever to have levered six sixteen ounce billiard cues at the same time by their tips through ninety degrees to the horizontal is W. J. (Bill) Hunt of Darwen, Lancashire. Christ – perhaps I should go for the billiard cues.

One more shot at my personal record – ninety-three pounds.

As he tries, MARIE *comes in from work. He raises the bar to his chest, and is struggling desperately to get it over his head.*

Marie Oo – should you be doing that, Stephen, your leg'll snap again.
Stephen I'm strengthening my leg.
Marie Well you'll shatter your spine.
Stephen I won't, I won't. (*Fails*) Oh, look, Ma, I was all set to equal my all-time best there. You interfered with my breathing . . .
Marie Sorry, love – have you have your tea?
Stephen Raw cabbage and Pure Lemon Juice.
Marie Oh – then you'll take some black pudding and bacon then?
Stephen (*goes and consults a chart*) Er – Er – I'll look at my chart. It doesn't mention black puddings one way or the other – better not, eh?

Marie Are you weight lifting or weight watching?

Stephen No, it's my Health and Efficiency Muscleman's Power-Intake Co-ordinator. It must be obeyed in every detail.

Marie I see.

Stephen So could you get me some yams – just four ounces?

Marie What happens if I don't – do you wither away?

Stephen I'll never equal Vasili Alexeev of the USSR.

Marie Have you done your homework?

Stephen You look as if you could shift a couple of hundredweight, Ma.

Marie Shut up and lay the table. Where's Val?

Stephen Dunno. Er – better not risk black pudding, eh?

Marie Black pudding is pure pig's blood, fried – it has the same effect as yams –

Stephen What?

Marie It fills your belly – now shift that, before I throw it out the window.

Stephen Go on then – let's see you. That could be a world record: heaviest weight ever thrown through a window by a woman.

Marie I'll shift it myself.

Enter VALERIE *and* SEYMOUR, *him very flowery, her quite nervous of the occasion.*

Valerie Oh – hello, er, Mother. I brought Seymour home for a minute while I get changed – hope you don't mind.

Marie Oh no, love, that's lovely – come in, Seymour, come in sit down. I'm afraid we're in here at the moment, it's all a bit of a mess. Sit down. Will you have some pig's blood and bacon?

Seymour Er – well –

Valerie Seymour's taking me out to dinner.

Marie Oh – haven't you had your dinner yet, it's tea-time? Oh evening dinner what a fool I am, how romantic. You'll take a cup of tea while you're waiting, I'll go and pop the kettle on.

Rushes out.

Valerie I won't be a minute, eh?

Seymour Yeah, that'll be cool, Val.

She goes, leaving STEPHEN *looking at* SEYMOUR.

Stephen Um: do you know where I could lay my hands on some – er – wait a minute – yams?

Seymour No.

Stephen Tricky one that, eh? (*Pause*) Could you lift that? (*Weight*)

Seymour No.

Stephen (*nods, understandingly, then*) Good job my dad's not here – he'd push your face in.

Seymour Would he?

Stephen He wouldn't like the look of you – say you were a pouf. Are you?
Seymour No.
Stephen Lift that then . . .

> SEYMOUR *looks helplessly around.* MARIE *comes back in.*

Marie Well, Seymour – it *is* nice to meet you.
Seymour Yeh.

> *Pause.*

Marie So you're in Promotion?
Seymour Yeh.
Marie That must be very interesting.
Seymour It's a bit of a drag, really.
Marie Very well paid though.
Seymour It comes and goes.
Marie You sound really fed up with it.
Seymour I want to make it as a DJ on Radio Valium.

> STEPHEN *laughs.*

Marie Would you feel happy doing that?
Seymour For a while.

> *Pause.*

Marie How much do you reckon you spend a week?
Seymour Hey, that's really heavy, really laying it on me, man –
Marie How much?
Seymour Well – I guess ninety, hundred pounds. Money doesn't go anywhere these days.
Marie So you're all right with the capitalist system then?
Seymour Wow – that's really political.
Marie Sorry – I'm just interested.
Seymour I'm not into that scene – politics – I believe they make people unhappy.
Marie Are you religious then?
Seymour Only if you think Eric Clapton really is God. No, I'm into love. And rock.
Marie Love? And rock?
Seymour And peace.
Marie Peace?
Seymour Listen, and learn, and hear your inner vactric sphere, with your inner inner ear.

> MUSIC. *He sings.*

> Mahatma Ghandi said it
> > Though his troubles never cease

Martin Luther King said
  Just before his sad decease
And Doctor Paisley said it
  To Mister Merlyn Rees

What'd they say – ? What did they say?

They said Peace, brother, Peace, man
Chorus   Peace brother, peace man –
Seymour Peace brother peace man
Chorus   Peace brother peace man –
If you don't give me peace man
I'll go and call a p'lice-man
And then you'll have to give me lots of peace.
Seymour Now General Franco said it,
  As they screwed the old garrotte
And Richard Nixon said it
  When Cambodia got the lot
And even poor old Adolf,
  As half the world got shot.

So don't go causing trouble,
Hostility's all wrong
  Just take what's coming to you,
  The weak obey the strong
  And if you feel like fighting,
  Just listen to my song
What'd you say? What do you say?
Chorus I say peace brother, peace man,
    etc.
Seymour And if you find that peace man –
  Your joys will never cease man
  And that's the end of your hassles – oh yeah.
Marie Seymour – are you worth a hundred pounds a week?
Seymour Do you know what Tony Blackburn's getting?
Marie I don't care. You're just trying to get rich and famous. There are quite
  a few people like you, aren't there – and we're all supposed to think
  you're wonderful. But really you get your money from selling things –
  that's your line, and your Dad's isn't it? Using sexy dollies to con money
  out of people who've had to work for it. Well my daughter's not just a
  sugar-plum fairy to titillate men's fantasies, you know –

Enter VALERIE *done up for going out to dinner, rather like a sugar-plum
fairy.*

Wrong again, Marie Arnold.

Valerie Shall we shoot off, then, Seymour?

Seymour Yeah –

Valerie Tara then – Mother. Here, Stephen, don't bar the door again tonight.

Stephen Too late. The horse has bolted.

Valerie I'm not working tomorrow till afternoon, so I won't rush back – OK?

Marie Val – don't be *too* late, love – (*whispers*) not with him.

Valerie Don't insult my friends or I'll be out of this house.

Marie Go on then – Good-bye Seymour – one thing I'll say for you – you've certainly been eating your crusts.

Seymour Yeh. (*At* STEPHEN) I wash behind my ears too, man. Peace little brother. Bye now.

MARIE *sees them off.*

Stephen Probably a City supporter – (*Sings*) You'll never walk again – (*Goes to weights*) Come on, you – Shazam! (*Lifts it over his head. Delight fades fast*) How the hell do you get it down? Ma – Ma! Gives a hand, quick, my back's under superhuman pressure.

The bar starts going back over his head – he has no idea how to get it down. Panic.

MARIE *rushes back in, helps him down with it, etc.*

Marie Bloody lunatic!

Stephen My back! My back!

Marie Oh no. I'll crack your skull open if you've done your back. (*Weights crash on to floor*) Are you all right?

Stephen (*rises, triumphant*) My personal all-time greatest.

Marie Is your back all right?

Stephen Perfect.

Marie Good, cos I've had an idea.

Stephen What?

Marie *You* can cook the black pudding and bacon.

Stephen Aw, eh – my homework, my back, my calisthenics –

Marie Into the back kitchen, and take that bogey with you.

Stephen But –

Marie Do as I say – or you'll grow up like Seymour . . .

Stephen Will I?

Marie Bacon and black pudding.

Stephen Right – do you want an egg with it, I'm ace at fried eggs, what about some fried bread – yeah! Ace! You wait till you see this meal . . . (*Goes, dragging weights with him*)

VALERIE *comes back in for her handbag, simpers, goes.* MARIE *wonders.*

TONIGHT'S THE NIGHT

MARIE *sits*. MUSIC.

Marie Our Val's going to sleep with that lad, tonight. She couldn't have made it plainer. It's done something to my guts, the way she come in, then – the way she hit me in the face with it: I am about to have torrential sex with this young man . . . (*Sings*)

> Tonight is the night for Valerie,
> And I don't know why I'm sad
> I did the same quite happily
> With many's the likely lad.
>
> But some damn thing is upsetting me,
> And it's something I just can't mend –
> And a pain, right here, is telling me
> That something has come to an end.
>
> To watch them grow is wonderful
> It's great to set them free:
> It's just – when they're off it's good-bye to all
> Those years they've had from me.
>
> And now as she steps out strong and bold,
> The world is all fresh and new
> But for me, it's a sign saying: Getting old –
> And for once I know it's true.

MUSIC *carries on.*

Marie I want it to be *me* going off. I don't *feel* like the one who gets left behind, I don't *feel* like a mother who ought to be worrying about he. daughter. I feel like I felt when I was sixteen – exactly. Why aren't *I* going off stinking of scent and deodorant?

I'm not *that* old though. And I've still got Stephen. God help me. (*Gets up*) Here, Stephen, love, don't worry, I'll do that for you.

STEPHEN *rushes in, waving a frying-pan.*

Stephen No, no – they're coming on great, look at that – ace. You stay there Er – how many eggs, three?
Marie Just one.
Stephen Right, any minute now – oho . . .

Goes off, delighted with himself.

Marie Can't all be bad.
    (*Sings*)
        Tonight is the night for Valerie
        And I suppose I should be glad –
        I did the same quite happily
        With many's the likely lad.

        But when they've all gone leaving me
        With memories and pain –
        If my body's not deceiving me
        I shall start all over again.

And that's just what I did.

I started all over again. I didn't take up with a fella – I reckon I'd had enough of fellas for a year or two.

No. What I did – I got seized with this notion, suddenly, in the middle of the bacon and egg.

Goes to table where STEPHEN *is stuffing his face, and reading about muscles. She starts to eat, then stops.*

Stephen –
Stephen Sh – sh –
Marie I intend to investigate this capitalist system. Have you got any ten pees?
Stephen Thirteen inches round the bicep –
Marie That Sir Jules Spike. I'm going to ring him up.
Stephen (*measuring his bicep*) What?
Marie Guildford, Surrey, he lives. I shall get Directory Enquiries to track him down. Then I shall ring up and ask him what his explanation is – come on, we're going to the phone box on the corner.
Stephen Me?
Marie You're a man, aren't you? Get your jacket on.
Stephen I'm eating my tea.
Marie Put it in the oven with mine.
Stephen It'll lose its texture. I've worked on that.
Marie Look, if I don't go now, this minute, I'll never go, and we'll never know about the capitalist system.
Stephen Oh. Right.
Marie So we went. We crammed into this phone box, I got Sir Jules's number from Directory Enquiries who were very helpful, and I dialled it on STD. It was a woman that answered.

Pips. Coin in.

Is that Sir Jules Spike's residence?
Lady Spike It is – who may I ask is that calling?

Marie Mrs Marie Arnold on long distance, I want to ask him a few questions.

Lady Spike He's not available at the moment, Mrs Arnold. This is Lady Spike speaking – could I be of any assistance?

Marie Yes. Your husband controls my destiny – now: what's he got that's so special?

Lady Spike How amusing – are you a blackmailer?

Marie No – I work for him in one of his factories – so how much money has he got in the bank for example?

Lady Spike I'm sure I don't know, and if I did I certainly wouldn't tell you.

Marie Why not? I bet he's got millions: why does he have to have millions and folk like us nowt? Anyway – I've been reading about you in the papers.

Lady Spike Oh have you?

Marie (*sings*)

> You've one black Jag, and one grey Rolls,
> And my lad's shoes is full of holes.

Lady Spike I suggest you pay a visit to the cobblers, my dear.

Marie He's only got one pair of shoes to his name, so Cobblers to you, my dear.

> You've bought a château down in France –
> Will *I* get t'Blackpool – not a chance.

Lady Spike Package holidays to such places as the Costa Brava are *very* inexpensive.

Marie The Costa Brava might be cheap, it's the Costa Living I can't afford.

Lady Spike If that's the best you can do, Mrs Arnold, you'll have to get off the line.

Marie (*sings*)

> And now I hear you've a private jet
> It'll save you queuein' for t'bus in t'wet
> And all this comes from folk like me,
> That's worked your husband's factory.
> There's something wrong, and no mistake –
> So where's the cash we've helped to make?

Lady Spike Are you a little jealous of my husband's success, perhaps?

Marie No. I'm interested in how the capitalist system works – it's my hobby . . .

Lady Spike Ah. Then I'll explain. It's quite easy.

Intro. to her SONG.

> All human kind is frail,
> Achievement is so rare,
> And yet we must not fail
> For progress we must dare
>
> To rouse the wrath of lesser men
> By rich rewards to others when

> They show the right intentions
> Invent the right inventions,
> For when a man's inventive
> He needs the right incentive . . .

It works by giving people *incentives* my dear. What drives a man to ever greater efforts but – well – money?

Marie Is it?

Lady Spike Look at the doctors, my dear, the great surgeons, the heart-specialists, the geniuses who save little children from untold suffering and agony – what possible reason could they have for doing what they do if it's not sixty thousand a year?

Marie But your husband isn't a brain-surgeon – he's just a great big boss . . .

Lady Spike Ah, but every businessman, in his way, is a Scott of the Antarctic – a pioneer:

(*Sings*)

> All human kind is frail,
> So one must organise –
> Though most are bound to fail
> Some have the enterprise
> To raise a business off the ground
> To make its profits safe and sound
> To take upon their shoulders
> The cares of their shareholders
> And when a man's succeeded
> Rewards are all that's needed.

Marie Well, yes, if he's clever and got something going, fair enough, he's done well, we should all wish him to have a decent wage for the rest of his life – but why must he build up millions of pounds, and keep robbing and cheating to get millions and millions more?

Lady Spike Ah, but that's the key to the whole capitalist system that you're so interested in, it's absolutely vital:

(*Sings*)

> All human kind is frail
> But those who know the score,
> If they don't go to jail
> Get more and more and more
> Of those with money to invest
> The ruthless man invests the best
> For men with human pity
> Would mess up all the City,
> D'you think we'd be in clover?
> The Japs would take us over . . .

So my husband has to make millions and be ruthless and drive you and your kind into misery to protect the British economy, Mrs

Arnold – he doesn't want to, really – he'd much rather walk the dog over the golf course twice daily – but he *has* to: you should be feeling sorry for him, really – I am. You can live in a world of fantasy, believing in justice and fair shares for all – he has to do battle with reality – the disintegrating pound, the American challenge, the Japanese invasion, the ever-growing power of the oil sheiks – it's a nightmare to Sir Jules, day in, day out. So don't bother to ring again unless to express your gratitude and admiration: Good-bye, Mrs Arnold.

Marie But Lady Spike –

Lady Spike Yes?

Pips go. MARIE *stuffs more money in.*

Marie Do you think it's the best way to go about things?

Lady Spike But it works.

Marie For some.

Lady Spike The proof of the pudding is in the eating my dear. I'm off to sink my gnashers into my profiterolle – if you don't like your prunes, spit them out –

Hangs up. Musical tail. Bows. Goes.

Stephen What did she say?

Marie She said I was to spit out my prunes. What kind of an answer was that? It seems her husband doesn't want to drive us into misery but he's got to in case all them foreigners come and drive us into misery. So he must be worried about the capitalist system as well: it's not doing anybody any good, really. So why don't we get rid of it?

Stephen That food'll be ruined.

Marie Stephen, I'd like to talk to a wise man.

Stephen Go on then. (*Offering himself*)

Marie No – do you know one?

Stephen Ah. Vasili Alexeev of the U Double SR must be wise.

Marie No, here.

Stephen Here? If he was a wise man, he'd have left here.

Marie There must be someone.

Stephen I'll think about it. (*Goes*)

Marie And there was! Stephen said his history teacher was standing as Labour candidate at the next election, so I thought – that's it, the party of the working-man, he *must* know the answers – so I told Stephen to bring him home one night after school – and he did.

Kitchen. STEPHEN *comes in with* CLEGHORN, *who enters singing.*

Cleghorn A – a – ah –
    I've received a short note:
    A – a – ah
    That your vote is afloat . . .

> We can't have voters all at sea
> I trust – that soon madame – you'll vote for me.

Cleghorn here, your Labour candidate, I understand you people, I'm from a lower-class family myself . . .

Marie Hello, Mr Cleghorn, thanks for coming round.

Cleghorn I know I'm not your MP yet, but you and I can soon see to that, and for a foretaste of things to come: What's your problem, Mrs – er – Arnold? Personal? Don't be shy, I'll do my best.

Marie Well – it's nothing really – it's just to do with my hobby.

Cleghorn Never mind, never mind, nowt's too trivial.

Marie Well – how do you go about smashing the capitalist system?

Cleghorn (*sings*)
> Ah – a – ah
> That's a dangerous note
> A – ah – ah
> And it's getting my goat
> The situation is delicate
> I trust that you will appreciate
> We cannot be precipitate –
> We must protect the Welfare State.

Marie I've had a taste of that, your Welfare State – it's not bad, you've done quite well in some ways – but from what I can see it's the capitalist system that's mucking it all up.

Cleghorn Softly softly catchee monkey, Mrs Arnold. In our country we have employers and workers, as in all democratic countries. BUT, thanks to our Mother of Parliaments, we have achieved a certain balance of power, a certain equilibrium of pressures, a certain stability of forces, as of two drunk men leaning against each other. But if one lurches, both will fall. Do you follow me?

Marie I follow you.

Cleghorn We can't just smash the capitalist system – the CBI would never agree –

Marie What's the CBI?

Cleghorn Er – the bosses: now we on the Left must appreciate that they represent a very important sector of our society, as do the financiers of the City, and it would be grossly unfair, manifestly unjust, indeed preposterously undemocratic to go against their wishes.

Marie If they don't like it, it's us against them isn't it? And there's more of us than them – so who's side are you on?

Cleghorn A – a – ah
> A detestable note –
> A – a – ah:
> Now you're rocking the boat
> To govern we need full consent

Of all good men of good intent
The British voter's quite content
With compromise for government.

The average voter here is more politically mature than the hot-headed teenagers of places like Chile and Portugal and Clay Cross. (*Shudders*) They don't want a party of sectional interests – they want a party of *all* the people – so that's what we are.

Marie So are the Conservatives.

Cleghorn And the Liberals. And the Scottish Nationalists. And the National Front. We *all* represent *all* the people.

Marie So what makes you lot different?

Cleghorn We, dear lady, are super subtle socialists. You may not even notice, but little by little, brick by brick, reform by reform, we shall do away with injustice, inequality and the Channel Tunnel, till one proud day we shall be the most radical country in NATO.

Marie But you're not going to scrap the system?

Cleghorn Out of the question. We'd lose the middle-class vote. Well, Mrs Arnold, it's been agreeable chatting with you, but I have to speak at the Junior Chamber of Commerce Annual Dinner tonight, so I must dash off and change.

Marie Just one minute – why don't your voters force you to do something?

Cleghorn A – a – ah
That's a note of despair
A – a – ah
Cos they don't really care.
They watch the news on BBC
They watch the ads on ITV
They read the press we must keep free
They're all confused, they're all at sea
And that's the way for Harold and me.

Goes.

Marie Stephen, do you think I'm mad?

Stephen No. What's for tea?

Marie Here – your turn to cook. It's beans on toast.

Stephen Wait till you see this toast . . .

STEPHEN *goes off.*

Marie Well I didn't get much joy out of Mr Cleghorn, did I? I think I scared him witless. But he did set me off thinking. I decided I'd better have a word with the bosses of the newspapers – so I rang one of them up . . . It was costing me a fortune in Ten Pees.

MISS WILLIAMS *comes on chained to a desk, answers her phone.*

Could I speak to Lord Leverbroom?

Williams I'm afraid he lives in Switzerland. I'm his assistant, can I help you?

Marie Yes. (*Sings*)

    Your paper tells us every day
    Just what to think and what to say
    Who says what facts you must select?
    Who says what facts you must reject?
    Who says what headlines scream with rage?
    Who says what never hits the page?
    And who says we are deaf and blind
    Who gave you t'right to rule my mind?

Williams Oh dear – we often get asked that question, dear Miss or Missus – and the answer is perfectly simple – whatever is newsworthy is worthy to be news – that's our sole criterion.

Marie Look, because I'd read your paper on and off for twenty years, when I went into my factory I almost refused to join the union, I nearly died when I met a shop-steward, and I'd rather have starved to death than gone on strike – I really must congratulate you, you did a grand job on me.

Williams Thank you.

Marie But now I know different. You weren't exactly telling me lies, one by one – it's just, what all you said added up to – that was a lie. And millions of people believe it. What possible reason can you have for doing that? What's your proprietor Lord What's his name up to?

Williams (*sings*)

    Our dear proprietor (What a man!)
      Is struggling every day:
    And what's his struggle for? (If he can!)
      To make his paper pay
    For the printers and their unions dictate
    If our paper stands or falls
    We've modernised too late too late –
    They've got us by the balls
    So if we bash the unions (Don't be soft)
    It's not a big surprise
    We need to spread confusion (Bash the Left)
    Survival is the prize.

Marie Are you part of the capitalist system as well?

Williams Oh, come come, Madame, what an ugly phrase – no, no we're above politics – like the Queen – dispassionate, impartial observers of life's gurgling ebb and flow – but we do believe in Britain – and that means Britain in all her glory and greatness – we find that is what our readers wish us to believe in.

(*Sings*)

    For British folk are proud (as they come)
    Of Britain's former might

So we proclaim it aloud (Bang the Drum)
    Each day in black and white
For the virtue of a patriotic call
    Defying wogs and frogs –
To a people who've no empire at all
    Who are going to the dogs
Is to feed our fantasies (Thin Red Line)
    And to make our bosoms swell
This national disease (Ninety-Nine)
    Will help our paper sell.

And we serve it up as the British public wishes us to serve it up – otherwise they wouldn't buy our papers – would they? So don't accuse us of printing trash – it's the trash the readers want to read. If you want to change the newspapers, change the readers.

Marie But they'll never change while they're reading the muck you're putting out. How come when there's a strike it's always us that's wrecking the economy, never the bosses?

Williams Ah – a fanatic. You'll have to ring off now, anonymous serf of the Kremlin, and call back after you've brain-washed the British population – but you're going to find it difficult – we British are not easily taken in by lies, distortion, biased reporting, sly propaganda – we have minds of our own, thank the Lord, and you socialists are all doped-up, lice infested long haired wierdos with bullets in your bathroom, bomb factories in your cellars, and blacks in your attics, and spy radios hidden behind your copies of Lenin, and miniature cameras in your Mao badges, so you can destroy our democracy, shoot the Queen, blow up the House of Commons, radio your masters in Moscow then take photographs of us all dying: so Chairman Mao can stick them in his album – but you will not succeed – the British press will be there to make sure no white Britishers will ever again be taken in by propaganda, of any sort.
(*Sings*)
    The world you watch on the news (Ev'ry day)
        In the press and radio
    Is a world we pick and choose (For our pay)
        A world it's safe to show.

    For the media-men with camera and pen
    Know *what* you all should see,
    So off they go and find it, then –
        It's simple as BBC

    We're dignified and wise (No you're not)
        Manipulate with skill
    We have no need for lies (Not a lot)
        For Truth obeys our will.

And that, dear miss or missus, is all you know on earth and all you need to know.

She goes.

PITTER PATTER

Marie My hobby was getting me nowhere – still it was better than ballroom dancing. Less sewing. By now, I'd really begun to get stuck into it – well, it riled me the way they all went on – as if I was mad even to think of questioning anything. And when I get riled, watch out.

I'd got nowhere with the bosses, nowhere with the Labour feller, and nowhere with the press – in desperation I turned to God – I made an appointment with the young curate – well, I lay in wait for him on the street corner. I didn't want him in the house, 'cos once you've let 'em in, you can never get shot of them. It was a dark November evening . . .

Mood music.

Young Curate, MR CHRIS PLUM, *walks contemplatively along the street.* MARIE *pounces on him.*

Psst! Vicar! Eh, you!

Mr Plum Jumping Jesus – you scared the shit out of me.

Marie Oo, should you be using language like that?

Mr Plum Ha, God understands. Besides, we sky pilots have been too far from the language of the people in times past – creates an unhealthy gulf between us and them. I make a practice of foul language on council house estates, brings you nearer to the people's guts.

Marie Oh.

Mr Plum Did you want something? I don't normally do guidance on the street.

Marie It won't take a minute. I saw you go into Mrs O'Rourke's house, so I didn't think you'd be long . . . Would you mind if I ask you a question?

Mr Plum We're out among the people, you know – and this is a prime example of exactly *why* we should be. Chap's walking along a dark, filthy, low-class street, and bloody bugger – out steps a woman with a question.

Marie I do wish you'd moderate your language.

Mr Plum Just to make you feel at home.

Marie D'you know, I don't think I'll bother.

Mr Plum No, no, you must – I'm terribly well qualified. I've got a First in Divinity at Oxford and I was mugged at Wapping.

Marie No – on your way – it wouldn't be fair.

Mr Plum For Christ's sake ask me a Goddam question – it's dreadful, dreadful, we even have to bribe people to ask us questions on television these days.

Marie All right – if it'll give you pleasure: now: the capitalist system – that's my subject, right? It makes people cheat and rob each other, turns men and countries against each other, and it's unjust, corrupt and evil: how come you Christians put up with it?

Mr Plum (*ecstatic*) Oh Doctor Coggan – if only you were here now – I feel I'm going to burst into song.

Marie Get yourself a microphone then or we shan't hear a word with all the seraphim and cherrybums over there.

Mr Plum (*sings*)

> In modern times the world is full
>> Of grasping, greed and strife
> But in this storm there comes a lull
>> Let's contemplate this life:
> The flesh is all, throughout the land
>> The spirit is denied –
> We never know just where we stand
>> We're never satisfied:
>
> But what does it matter
> If the rain comes pitter-patter
>> And the North Winds howl round your head?
> For rich and for poor
> Just a few years more
>> And we'll one and all be dead.

Marie We'll all be dead? Oh no! It's what happens before that I'm interested in. I might have known.

Mr Plum A – a, not so predictable, not so dismissable. After-life. Life after death. What does it mean? We modern theologians have come to a deeper, more humanistic understanding of that ancient pagan fantasy; for it is an image – no more, no less – for just as death gives a meaning to life, so our image of our place in a mythical after-life gives meaning to our random, incoherent, otherwise meaning-less existence in this life: of our true place in this life. That's what it's *for*, you see – that's its function.

And what do we learn of this life, if we view it from the perspective of an after-life? We see that it needs two things: order, and spirituality. And we cannot have one without the other. Spirituality to raise the level of our own beings above the brutish and into contact with that within us which we call divine. Spirituality, also, to transform our relationships with those about us from envy and distrust, into love and service. But for such spirituality to flourish in security, we must have order. Confucius knew. Plato knew. Christ had it knocked off. Render unto Caesar those things which are Caesar's. What does that mean? It means the world must have order – perhaps not perfect, nothing is perfect in this life, but recognised and adhered to. Now what did Cardinal Bourne mean when he said: We owe obedience to God, and the authority of God Himself is vested in the government, therefore we owe obedience to the government? Aha, some cynic will sneer, so God lives in 10 Downing Street. No no, look deeper. Every human being demands an authority set above him, be it a father, a priest, a headmaster, or Karl Marx. And this demand for authority, the power that will create order, is projected on to a non-existent person called God. So when we say God vests his authority in the Queen or the Prime Minister, or the Governor of the Bank of England, or the capitalist system – we are being tautological: we mean – that's what we invented God for – to express our desire for these men to wield authority, to create an order out of our chaos, to imprint our society with a pattern – why? To create a secure framework for our lonely, individual spirituality to go to town in. So *we* can find personal salvation. Do you follow me?

Marie I think so.

Mr Plum So: a family needs a father. A factory needs a boss. Politicians need a Prime Minister. The Bank of England needs a Governor. And a country needs a Queen. So we can all love one another, and flourish in the spirit. That's why we need a capitalist system, dear lady. And we can all go to Heaven forgiving each other for what it does to us. Oh Doctor Coggan, you're wonderful.

Marie Hang on, hang on. Our family hasn't got a father, and we get on all right.

Mr Plum Well, of course there *can* be –

Marie And I don't give a bugger if the Queen drops dead, or the Prime Minister come to that. And as for the factory – all right, we need some sort of management, but not a thieving millionaire and a load of shareholders sitting on their bums taking money out of our wages every week.

Mr Plum Holy Fuck: Spirituality, dear lady – materialism is for the brutes.

Marie How come it's materialism, when *I* want money, and Godliness when they get it? All that patter – who's paying you? The Queen and the government and the Bank of England, I bet, and you're stuffing people's heads with rubbish of all descriptions just to shut them up.

Mr Plum No – no no. What we have, is what people want. I service the people's fantasies, just like a mechanic services their motor cars, that is all. Make them content with what they have chosen.

Marie But it's impossible to choose anything else with people like you around.

Mr Plum Then you'll have to get rid of me. And I won't give up without a struggle.

Marie You are my enemy.

Mr Plum (*sings*)
>Theology, philosophy
>>All serve the status quo,
>Apologise for history
>>Explain what we all know

If you would change society
　We'll kick and scream and fight
The watch dogs of authority
　Will prove that might is right.

Chorus But what does it matter, etc.

He goes as he sings chorus.

Mr Plum Good-night. God bless. Do you know I think I'll mention this incident to the bastarding bishop.

Goes.

Marie That's the end of seeking wisdom. *They* were all doing just great, the folk I went to see. But I wasn't. I still had all this energy, and curiosity, but where was it getting me? Nowhere.

Then our Stephen left school – oh dear – couldn't wait, sixteen years, one day, and out. Now there's sod all for him to do. What a waste. And he's getting a bit restless, one way and the other – well, sixteen's a restless age, isn't it? I'll have to keep an eye on him, or there'll be trouble there.

THE WAITING GAME

Music in – whistling. The street.

TWO GIRLS *stagger across on high platform shoes, aimless.* STEPHEN *comes on after them, stops, shrugs.*

Stephen Roamin' round the streets of a winter's night
Without a penny to my name
Laughing at the lasses' big clogs, what a sight,
Playing the waiting game.

I'm sweet sixteen and never had a grope,
But I'll get one just the same
I'm sweet sixteen and my only hope
Is playing the waiting game.

I'm all dressed up and nowhere to go,
The club's all dull and tame,
I'm sweet sixteen and the pubs all know
So I'm playing the waiting game.

I could use some cash but I can't get a job
Sorry, son, what a shame –
And my ma won't lend me her last ten bob
So I'm playing the waiting game.

On Friday night when the cash rolls in
I'll be off to stake my claim
See that lass called Lynn, gonna fill her up with gin,
Then it's on with the mating game.

Band   Sweet sweet sixteen
A soul that's pure and clean –
No work no money
And acne isn't funny –
When you're Sweet sweet sixteen.

STEPHEN *has gone to chat up one of the girls, comes back dismayed.*

Stephen   She says my face makes her want to spew,
Can't say I set her all aflame,
There's nowt to do, so Up you Too –
And back to the waiting game.
(*Speaks*) I think I'll go and kick some old lady's head in.

He goes.

Marie Poor Stephen, he does have a hard time. They reckon he'll be lucky to get a start in eighteen months – what a waste. I ask you. Still, I mustn't start on again – it just infuriates me, the whole thing. And thinking about it, and asking about it, and worrying about it does you no good at all. I suppose the only answer is to *do* something about it – but what?
The one thing all those people were saying was that they kept the system going because we wanted it. They're a bunch of liars, 'cos they were all doin' their best to stop folk wantin' anything else. But all the same – if people don't think about it, like I didn't for thirty-four years, they won't know whether they want it or not. That's where it all points, my little trail – lots of little arrows all pointing at me – and her – and her.

LITTLE ARROWS BIG BOW

Back in the factory. JOSEY, FRANCES *are there working.* MARIE *joins them.*

Josey Did you see that on telly last night? They were in this shop, and a yeller feller comes in and he asked for a lain-coat and they didn't know what he wanted till this other feller said he was Japanese and the Japanese have difficulty getting their tongue round their Rs. Do you get it? Our Harry didn't half laugh, kept goin' tee hee all night. I'm glad he enjoyed it 'cos he stopped in special to watch the football and it was abandoned 'cos of fog. I feel abandoned 'cos of fog sometimes. Still – what got me – we got to bed early, you know, and that, and right in the middle it was all passionate sort of, well quiet, and he starts rolling about laughing about the Japanese.

MARIE *and* FRANCES *laugh with* JOSEY.

Frances Big George is paying us a visit today.

Marie Who's Big George?

Josey Feller from the union. He's taken over the negotiations about the guaranteed wage and bonus agreement from that other twit.

Marie Oh great – will he get something done then?

Frances By the end of the century.

Josey He's quick in some ways, slow in others, is George.

Marie I've never met a big union feller before – is he like Jimmy Reid?

Josey Not exactly. More like Al Read.

Frances You'll see.

Marie I suppose I will.

> *They work on, then* MARIE *remembers.*

Marie Do you remember I told you about our Val going out with this freaky bloke? Well this morning, when I got up, she wasn't there. Hadn't come back all night. (*Reactions*) I don't know what to do about it. She's eighteen now, I know, but – well, I wouldn't mind so much if I could bring myself to like him.

Josey What's his name again?

Marie Seymour. Seymour Bell.

Josey Oo, hey up, that name rings summat. No, I'm not joking, is his Dad in clubs and girls with a big house over the park?

Marie Sounds like him, why?

Josey That's where they show blue films and have orgies.

Marie What? (*Laughs*) How do *you* know?

Josey I was told Harry went to one, and I copped him one with the bread board, he had seven stitches in his head and now his hair won't grow – just there.

Marie Are you sure?

Josey Ten quid for watching the blue movies and the orgy's on the house.

Marie I can feel prickles running all over my skull.

Josey Don't fret – that's the old feller; I'm sure Seymour's a nice enough young man.

Marie Are you? I'll tell you tomorrow.

> *Hooter blows. As they stop work,* GEORGE *rushes in.*

George Just in time, girls, perfect timing as ever. Hello Josey – how's tricks?

Josey I'm thinking of selling you my body, George – what am I worth?

George Give us a free sample, and I'll post you an estimate.

Frances Come on George, what's gone wrong this time?

George Aw, Fran, eh – desirable as a juicy pear in the Sahara Desert.

Frances Come on, what have you managed? And if not, why not?

George You girls, you don't appreciate your own succulence – do you? No. Er – we can't reach agreement.

Frances and Josey Oh no. Not again.

Frances This is getting ridiculous, George, it's been going on for two years, this daft game – we want some results, my girls are not satisfied.

George Aw – have to see what we can do about that, eh girls?

Frances Knock it off, lover boy.

Marie Why is he going on as if we were a joke? That's insulting behaviour that.

George Who are you?

Frances This is Marie – she's only been here a year and a half, you won't have met her. (*To* MARIE) This is George, your union representative.

Marie Are they all like you?

George No – unfortunately they're not, but give us a postal ballot and we'll soon get rid of the wreckers.

Frances Now then, let's have it – what have you settled for?

George No, honest, nothing. They say we don't represent the work-force. There's a hundred and ninety girls on piece-work, and only seventy-two in the union – it's your fault, girls, you should have been whipping them in ten at a time. It puts me in a daft position.

Frances How can we get them all in the union when they sack half of them every three months?

George That's your problem.

Frances It's not. It's yours – that's what you're here to put a stop to. You don't need everybody in the union, George, you're messing about – go in there and tell them: piece-work is over. Give 'em that wage rate thing Big Alice worked out, tell 'em that's the pay, and the shop-steward'll negotiate the bonus for every new job.

George No, no. That they won't have – they insist on setting the bonus rates themselves, they refuse to negotiate ever with shop-stewards.

Frances Oh, so you have been discussing with them?

George Purely informally.

Marie They insist, they refuse – doesn't sound like an informal discussion to me.

George And they laughed at the wage rates. Well, we were pitching it a bit high . . .

Frances No, we weren't: them rates is what they're paying for this work in Hemel Hempstead, we checked.

George They'll never accept them – but don't worry, I'll be tough and fearless.

Marie When you're talking to them – do you have to put your hand up if you want to go to the lav?

George (*to* MARIE) Are you a union member?

Marie Yes.

George Then shut up.

Marie No, I won't. I think we should get all the girls together – in the union or not, at dinner-time today, and we should tell them we're being pushed around, and laughed at: then get them all out on strike, and not come back till we've got what we want.

George Strike? But these parts are needed – you go on strike and there's men, with families, out of work.

Marie Oh. And what about the export drive? Tell us about that.

George Eh? Anyway, Head Office would never make it official, so you'd be back in a fortnight, smashed.

Marie Would we?

George Yes. And even if you weren't, they'd just get another load of women from the Labour Exchange and wheel them in.

Marie Not if we were standing at the gate, they wouldn't.

George Are you a Trot?

Marie A what? No, whatever it is, I'm not. I'm just fed up being pushed around by the capitalist system. I want it scrapped, it's wrong, and I think we can do better, and I've come to the conclusion that the best place to start is here, right here.

George She's mad.

Marie What are you doing about smashing the capitalist system?

George At the moment, Mrs Lenin, I'm doing my best to keep it going so we're not all out of work . . .

Marie Wonderful. That's great news down the dole queue that is. I must tell our Stephen, he'll be impressed by your strategy.

George You're an anarchist.

Marie Stop sticking labels on me and start doing your job. You can't help us by keeping capitalism going – surely that's not what the unions are all about. *You* should be showing a bit of initiative, not sitting on every sign of trouble, and licking the boss's backside. So shove off, and we'll organise a mass meeting, and we'll tell you what to say if we think you're capable of saying it. If not, we'll say it ourselves. Won't we, girls?

Frances You asked for that, George.

George Women. Adventurists. Ultra-lefts. Anarchists. What you lot need is discipline. And that's what you're going to get.

He goes.

Josey Seems to be having difficulty getting his tongue round his Rs.

Marie Sorry girls, did I go too far?

Frances It's about time somebody told him.

Enter POTSHOT *with trolley.*

Josey Oh, here's Potshot back again. Come for your holidays, little one?

Potshot It is Easter time. The Son of Man is risen and walks amongst you. I need the money.

Frances He's not changed, has he?

Josey Not even his T-shirt . . .

Potshot It is delightful to see you ladies again. (*To* MARIE) Greetings, comrade, how goes the revolution?

Marie You just missed it. I gave our big union bloke his cards, nearly thumped him one.

Potshot Ah – you got a whiff of class collaboration in your nostrils then? Hardly surprising.

Marie Listen, Potshot, I've been doing this one-woman uprising all on my own for too long. I think I'd better join something: how do you go about that then?

POTSHOT *takes a deep breath*

Josey Oh, he's going to make a speech.

Potshot Don't mock, Josey, or I'll have your knickers off. Sorry about that piece of male chauvinism.

Marie Come on, then . . .

Potshot There are, as you may be aware, a number of organisations working to replace bourgeois society with various forms of socialism. You must join one of them. As there are several, you will be confronted with a choice. I must warn you that choosing your revolutionary organisation should not be done in the way a Mayfair lady selects a brand of lipstick. Don't choose the prettiest or the reddest – though it might be an idea to choose one that you can wear in public without feeling too embarrassed. But you must choose, and join, and work, or you will remain confused and apathetic, and a joy to Sir Jules Spike.

I have made my choice. I certainly intend to influence you to join my particular groupuscule or sect. However, there are other ways of working for socialism. This I admit: some would not, but every movement has its fascists. Eventually there will be one revolutionary organisation which will be created and controlled by the working class of Britain. To create that, we must all give everything. If we do – it will succeed. I shall draw up a list of names and addresses, newspapers and books. Comrade, good luck.

Marie Thank you.

Potshot Now I must off to the Mount, I have a sermon to deliver on it, and some vertical take-off to indulge in. Farewell.

He goes.

Josey Well – you are going to land yourself in trouble.

Marie Am I?

Josey Potshot says every time a copper sneezes, they raid his room to look for bottles of poisonous germs.

Marie I've got to do *something*. And the first thing I'm going to do is organise that meeting tomorrow dinner-time, come on, quick – twelve-thirty in the loading bay, right? If we split up we can get round everybody in ten minutes or so.

Frances Wait a minute. The shop-stewards' committee calls the meetings round here – you go and see Big Alice and she'll see you all right.

Marie Right. I will. Eh – should we ask the men?
Josey Why not? They must be good for something.

Hooter.

Marie Oh shut up. Here, tell 'em I've got food poisoning . . .

She goes. Hooter ends. They go off.

MARIE *comes on with basket, on her way home. Ballad music quietly behind:*

Big Alice listened to me, said I was crazy, then she went round the committee members, and persuaded them I was right. The meeting's not tomorrow, it's next Wednesday. But there will be a meeting, and if I can pluck up the courage, I'm going to speak.

Potshot waylaid me at dinner time, and give me a stack of papers, a lot of addresses, twenty books I've got to read, and an earful of arguments about his group, and the X Y Z, and the BBC ML – I can't begin on that, they all seem to be fighting each other. However, I'm taking all the stuff home to read; it's in here with the sausages. But first, I want to see our Val. If she's back. I'll give her what for. (*Goes off*)

WHERE WE START FROM

Kitchen.

Enter JACK, *with kitbag and presents. He puts them down, looks around. Sees dirty plates on table, socks on chair. He sits down on top of the socks, and lights his pipe.* STEPHEN *comes in, wonders who it is, decides:*

Stephen Oh – seen my socks?
Jack Stephen. Just the same, eh? Here –
Stephen What time is it?
Jack (*throws him a small parcel*) Here –
Stephen What's that?
Jack A present from Piraeus –
Stephen Piraeus – I thought you got that on your gums.
Jack Open it. Glad to see me back?
Stephen No. What time is it?
Jack Open the bloody present – it's a watch.
Stephen Oh. I'll just go and get my shoes. (*Goes off*)

JACK *smokes, filling the place with smoke.*

Jack Grand welcome.

MARIE *comes in.*

Marie Christ, it's Jack.
Jack Hello, love. Oh it's good to see you – you look just the same.

Marie Do I? How long you been smoking a pipe then?

Jack Year or so – should be a clay one, eh, for a seafarer . . .

Marie Have you had a good time, in all them places?

Jack None so good as I've had here love. I mean that.

Marie Oh. Have you, d'you think you've come back?

Jack (*nods*) I kept thinking about you. I'm sorry for all the misery and sadness I must have caused you. I won't ever go away again.

Marie Won't you?

Jack I've made a vow.

Marie Oh shit.

Jack Don't bother about my tea, Marie – just sit down and relax. It's home again. Here – that's for you – from Singapore: and it's very unusual. The natives wear 'em.

Marie Oh no.

Jack Go on, it's yours. I thought about you, girl, all over the seven seas – I've seen the world, I tell you – and there's nowhere to beat England.

MARIE *cries.* JACK *puts his arm round her.*

That's right. You have a good cry.

Enter VALERIE, *she freaks with joy.*

Valerie Dad! Oh Dad, it's really you! (*He hugs her—looks at her.*)

Jack Val – you're – a young woman.

Valerie Yeh.

He hugs her again. MARIE *perks up.*

Marie Jack, put her down. Sit over there and shut up. I'll deal with you in a minute. Now then, miss – where've you been?

Valerie Only to London. Keep your hair on.

Marie And what do you know about Seymour's dad, and his house over the park?

Valerie It's where he lives.

Marie And carries on his business.

Valerie Aw look, Ma, can this wait till I've said hello to my dad? I haven't seen him for two years.

Marie I'll talk to you later.

Jack Needing a father's guiding hand, are you, Valerie? Oh – I'm sorry you've been without for so long.

STEPHEN *comes in.*

Stephen There's macaroni cheese in the oven, Ma – I've had mine. I'm going out.

Valerie Stephen! It's your dad!

Stephen Yeh, saw him.

Jack Christ, has the lad had to cook his own tea? Soon get this place in order, eh Val?

Valerie Yeh.

Stephen Will you?

Jack Look, lad – are you bearing me a grudge? If so, knock it off – I've said I'm sorry I left you all like that, and I'm back now and let's all get on together shall we? I can see the pair of you haven't had much of a helping hand in life, but that can soon be seen to.

Stephen Get out. You're not staying here.

Jack Oh God, I might have expected something like this. Now listen, Stephen, it's very clear to me you *need* a father round the place, so just calm down and behave yourself.

Stephen Or what?

Jack Are you threatening me?

Stephen Yes.

Jack How dare you?

Stephen Go away and come back when you're a human being.

Valerie Stop it, stop it!

Jack Stephen, get used to the idea. I've come back, to stay.

Marie You don't seem to remember, Jack, you didn't leave – I threw you out. For good.

Valerie Are you going to drive him out again? Are you?

Jack Look Marie, that with Alma – it was just stupidity – don't say you're still jealous about that.

Marie Jealous? About *that*? (*She laughs*)

Jack Can't you forgive and forget for once, woman?

Marie (*quietly*) It's got nothing to do with that, love. It didn't have much to do with that then. It's just – things have changed – attitudes, ways of looking at things.

Jack Well I haven't.

Marie No, I can see. Now let's get this straight – there might come a time when I'm prepared to take you on. I hope there will. But just now – I can't. I simply can't.

Jack What are you saying? What's come over you?

Marie Do me a favour, Jack – go.

Valerie Oh no.

Jack But I've got nowhere to stay. No one to cook my food, look after me.

Marie Exactly.

Jack I can't go. I've travelled seven thousand miles to be with you.

Marie The same seven thousand you travelled to get away from us: don't try that, Jack, it won't wash.

Stephen Thanks for the present, Dad – it was nice of you to remember us.

JACK *gets up.*

Valerie If he goes, I go.

Marie Not before I've had a word with you.

Jack Right. I see how it is now. Don't worry, I'm not stopping. You've turned into a hard, bitter, unnatural – I almost said woman. Here Val – for you. (*With tender sentiments, gives her a present*)

Valerie Wait for me, Dad – wait for me outside, I want to hear about where you've been, the beaches in Australia.

Jack I'll be in the Lion. Residents Lounge. (*To* MARIE) Whatever's happened to you, love? You're certainly not the girl I married.

Marie No. I'm not. Come back when you're prepared to find out who I am now. Not before.

JACK *goes.* STEPHEN, MARIE *and* VALERIE *sitting at table.*

Which way are you going to go, Stephen?

Stephen To the baths, I'm in the Breast Stroke Finals. I'm getting a bit old for swimming though . . . Do you know anybody with a set of golf-clubs?

Marie Go your ways.

Stephen Don't forget the macaroni cheese. (*Goes*)

Valerie I wasn't in London last night, Ma.

Marie Weren't you?

Valerie I was in that house; it was the first time, honest.

Marie Do you want to tell me about it?

Valerie (*shakes head*) I want – to hear from you. Will you talk to me?

MUSIC *in, as* MARIE *begins to talk.*

Singer   The time is pushing seven-thirty,
        The place a grotty town
    Where folks are clean and weather's dirty,
        And life's all grey and brown.
    Now we've come to the end of our story,
        Not much happened, that is true –
    If you want an end, we're sorry,
        The rest is up to you.

    Cos she's nobody,
    Nobody, nobody,
    Nothing to shout about –
    Now everybody's
    Somebody
    But she's just yobbo nowt, yobbo nowt, yobbo nowt.

END OF PLAY